MW01591790

# Table of Contents

# FREE GIFT!

In order to thank you for buying my book I am glad to present you
- BEST Delicious & Famous 1000 Recipes -

Please follow this link to get instant access to your Free Cookbook: http://booksquare.info/

# Introduction

Do you love fried food? If you're like many people out there, you love the taste of fried food but hate the thought of all the calories that you're consuming along with the deliciousness. The Airfryer is a game changer! You can cook your favorite fried foods and reduce calories to a percent of what they would be when cooked in a conventional frying device.

In this book, you'll discover new and somewhat familiar recipes to get you inspired and cooking!

# Breakfast

## Blueberry muffins

**Prep time: 10 minutes**
**Cooking time: 12 minutes**

### Ingredients:

- 1.5 cups of whole wheat flour
- 2 tablespoons of sugar (adjust if you prefer a sweeter tasting muffin)
- 2 teaspoons of baking powder
- A pinch of sea salt
- 2 tablespoons of coconut oil warmed to liquid
- 1 cup of milk (or coconut, almond, cashew or any other type of nutmilk)
- 1 egg
- 1 tablespoon of plain yogurt (coconut yogurt is fine for those avoiding lactose)
- A dash of vanilla extract or real vanilla powder (or scrape a vanilla pod)
- A handful of frozen blueberries

### Directions:

1. Combine all the dry ingredients (the flour, sugar, baking powder, sea salt, vanilla if in powdered form) in a bowl. Stir to evenly combine them.
2. Combine all of the wet ingredients in another bowl (the liquid coconut oil, milk, egg, yoghurt and vanilla extract if in liquid form). Whisk so the liquid is evenly combined.
3. In a large bowl, combine wet and dry ingredients. Use a hand mixer or a whisk to combine well. Fold in the blueberries evenly.
4. Put five muffin cups into the Airfryer. Pour in the mixture leaving space at the top of the cups for the muffins to rise.
5. Heat the Airfryer to 350 degrees F. Allow to "airfry" for 12 minutes and then check using a fork. (Stick the fork into a muffin, if the fork comes out clean, the muffins are ready). If necessary, or a slightly more browned look is desired, airfry for another 3 minutes.
6. Sprinkle with powdered sugar or top with honey if so desired.
7. Enjoy

# Raspberry walnut muffins
**Prep time: 10 minutes**
**Cooking time: 12 minutes**

## Ingredients:
- 1.5 cups of whole wheat flour
- 2 tablespoons of sugar (adjust if you prefer a sweeter tasting muffin)
- 2 teaspoons of baking powder
- A pinch of sea salt
- 2 tablespoons of coconut oil warmed to liquid
- 1 cup of milk (or coconut, almond, cashew or any other type of nutmilk)
- 1 egg
- 1 tablespoon of plain yogurt (coconut yogurt is fine for those avoiding lactose)
- A dash of vanilla extract or real vanilla powder (or scrape a vanilla pod)
- A handful of frozen raspberries
- 0.5 cup of chopped walnuts
- A tablespoon of real maple syrup (optional)

## Directions:
1. Combine all the dry ingredients (the flour, sugar, baking powder, sea salt, vanilla if in powdered form) in a bowl. Stir to evenly combine them.
2. Combine all of the wet ingredients in another bowl (the liquid coconut oil, milk, egg, yoghurt and vanilla extract if in liquid form). Whisk so the liquid is evenly combined.
3. In a large bowl, combine wet and dry ingredients. Use a hand mixer or a whisk to combine well. Fold in the walnuts and frozen raspberries taking care to evenly distribute them.
4. Put five muffin cups into the Airfryer. Pour in the mixture leaving space at the top of the cups for the muffins to rise.
5. Heat the Airfryer to 350 degrees F. Allow to "airfry" for 12 minutes and then check using a fork. (Stick the fork into a muffin, if the fork comes out clean, the muffins are ready). If necessary, or a slightly more browned look is desired, airfry for another 3 minutes.
6. Top with a drizzle of maple syrup or brown sugar.

# Egg and ham breakfast sandwich
**Prep time: 5 minutes**
**Cooking time: 6 minutes**

**Ingredients:**
- One roll of your choice, sliced in half (English muffin, kaiser bun, etc)
- 1-2 eggs
- 1-2 slices of ham
- A bit of butter

**Directions:**
1. Butter your sliced roll with butter on both sides.
2. Place the eggs in an oven safe dish. Whisk. (For a gourmet approach, add a pinch of salt, herbs such as oregano, dill, chives, etc)
3. Put the egg dish along with the roll and the ham. (Make sure the buttered sides of the roll are facing upwards). Airfry at 390 degrees F for six minutes.
4. Remove the ingredients. Put the egg and ham between the pieces of the roll and enjoy (top with whatever you like on your breakfast sandwich!)

**Tip**: pesto is a delicious and somewhat unexpected condiment for breakfast!

# Hash browns
**Prep time: 5 minutes**
**Cooking time: 16 minutes**

**Ingredients:**
- 2 cups cubed potatoes ( any type of potato will do)
- 2 tablespoons of olive oil
- Salt to taste

**Directions:**
1. Preheat the Airfryer to 360 degrees F.
2. Place the cubed potatoes in a bowl. Add the olive oil and coat evenly over the potatoes. (Stir and toss the mixture carefully.) Sprinkle with salt. (A tasty tip is to substitute conventional salt with garlic salt)
3. Put the potatoes into the Airfryer basket. Place inside the Airfryer and cook for 16-18 minutes depending on how golden brown you want your hash browns to be.
4. Remove from the Airfryer and enjoy with your favorite breakfast sandwich!

# Egg and cheese breakfast sandwich
**Prep time: 5 minutes**
**Cooking time: 6 minutes**

**Ingredients**:
- 1 roll of your choice, sliced in half (English muffin, kaiser bun, etc)
- 1-2 eggs
- 1-2 slices of cheddar cheese (swiss, provolone or any type of sliced cheese may be used here)
- A bit of butter

**Directions:**
1. Butter your sliced roll with butter on both sides.
2. Place the eggs in an oven safe dish. Whisk. (For a gourmet approach, add a pinch of salt, herbs such as oregano, dill, chives, etc.)
3. Put the egg dish along with the roll and the cheese into the Airfryer. (Make sure the buttered sides of the roll are facing upwards). Airfry for six minutes at 390 degrees F.
4. Remove the ingredients. Put the egg and cheese between the pieces of the roll and enjoy. Try tomato and avocado slices as a healthy and delicious addition to this warm breakfast sandwich.

# Peanut butter and banana breakfast sandwich
**Prep time: 5 minutes**
**Cooking time: 6 minutes**

**Ingredients**:
- 2 slices of whole wheat (or gluten free) bread
- About 2 tablespoons of peanut butter
- 1 sliced banana
- 1 teaspoon (approximately) of honey or maple syrup

**Directions:**
1. Evenly coat both sides of the bread with peanut butter. Add the sliced banana. A drizzle of honey or maple syrup makes for a wonderful consistency.
2. Heat the Airfryer to 330 degrees F. Place the sandwich inside and heat for 6 minutes.
3. Enjoy the gooey goodness of this warm breakfast sandwich!

# Spinach and cheese omelette

**Prep time: 5 minutes**
**Cooking time: 8 minutes**

**Ingredients**:
- 3 eggs
- 0.5 cup of shredded cheese (mozzarella, cheddar )
- 2 tablespoons of chopped fresh spinach (or thawed frozen spinach)

**Directions:**
1. Whisk the eggs. Place the eggs in a flat oven safe form.
2. Add the cheese and spinach. Do not stir.
3. Cook at 390 degrees F for 8 minutes in the Airfryer.
4. Check the consistency of the omelette. If a browner omelette is desired, cook for an additional 2 minutes.
5. Enjoy with bread, ketchup or any other condiments you prefer.

# Bacon and cheese breakfast pie

**Prep time: 5 minutes**
**Cooking time: 15 times**

**Ingredients**:
- 1 pre-made thin pastry crust (use croissant dough or another type of thin pastry dough, pre-made or make your own)
- 3 eggs
- 2 slices of fried bacon, chopped into small pieces
- 1 cup of shredded cheese

**Directions:**
1. In flat oven safe form, cut the pie crust to fit the form. (Simply cut off the edges hanging off the sides.)
2. Whisk the eggs in a mixing bowl.
3. Put the egg mixture into the pie crust form. Top with the cheese and the bacon.
4. Bake at 360 degrees F in the Airfryer for 15 minutes. Allow another 3 minutes if necessary.
5. Enjoy!

# Easy maple breakfast cakes (Airfryer pancakes)

**Prep time: 5 minutes**
**Cooking time: 8 minutes**

**Ingredients**:

- 1.5 cups flour (whole wheat, white)
- 3 tablespoons of maple syrup (adjust accordingly if you want sweeter cakes with a stronger maple taste)
- 2 eggs
- 0.5 cups milk

**Directions:**

1. Combine and mix the ingredients with a hand mixer. Preheat the Airfryer to 360 degrees F.
2. In a lightly greased oven safe flat form, pour enough batter in so that the batter is about one quarter of an inch in depth.
3. Cook the pancake for three minutes. Remove, and flip over the cake. Return to the Airfryer for another five minutes.
4. Repeat the process with the remaining batter.
5. Enjoy with maple syrup, whipped cream (extra decadent), or jam.

# Zucchini and cream cheese muffins

**Prep time: 10 minutes**
**Cooking time: 12-15 minutes**

**Ingredients**:
- 1.5 cups of whole wheat flour
- 2 tablespoons of sugar
- 1 teaspoon cinnamon
- 2 teaspoons of baking powder
- A pinch of sea salt
- 2 tablespoons of coconut oil warmed to liquid
- 1 cup of milk (or coconut, almond, cashew or any other type of nutmilk)
- 1 egg
- 1 tablespoon of plain yogurt (coconut yogurt is fine for those avoiding lactose)
- 0.5 cups shredded zucchini
- 1 tablespoon of cream cheese

**Directions:**
1. Combine all the dry ingredients (the flour, sugar, baking powder, cinnamon sea salt,) in a bowl. Stir to evenly combine them.
2. Combine all of the wet ingredients in another bowl (the liquid coconut oil, milk, egg and yoghurt. Whisk so the liquid is evenly combined.
3. In a large bowl, combine wet and dry ingredients. Use a hand mixer or a whisk to combine.
4. Stir in the shredded zucchini. Divide up the cream cheese into small pieces. Fold in the cream cheese, taking care to distribute evenly.
5. Put five muffin cups into the Airfryer. Pour in the mixture leaving space at the top of the cups for the muffins to rise.
6. Preheat the Airfryer to 350 degrees F. Allow to "airfry" for 12 minutes and then check using a fork. (Stick the fork into a muffin, if the fork comes out clean, the muffins are ready). If necessary, or a slightly more browned look is desired, airfry for another 3 minutes.
7. Sprinkle with powdered sugar or top with honey if so desired.

# English breakfast

**Prep time: 10 minutes**
**Cooking time: 25 minutes**

**Ingredients:**
- 2 eggs
- One sausage
- Two cups beans in tomato sauce
- One cup sliced and diced potatoes
- One tablespoon olive oil
- Salt to taste

**Directions:**
1. Preheat your Airfryer to 390 degrees F.
2. Crack the eggs onto an oven safe dish. Sprinkle with salt if desired.
3. Place the beans next to the eggs.
4. In a separate container, place the potatoes, and the tablespoon of olive oil. Use your hands to combine well. Sprinkle with salt if desired.
5. First place the potatoes in the Air fryer. Cook for 10 minutes.
6. Then place the form with the eggs and the beans. Cover the potatoes with parchment paper to separate.
7. Cook for an additional 10 minutes.
8. Cut the sausage into pieces and add to the dish with the beans and eggs.
9. Cook for another 5 minutes.
10. Serve with toast and coffee for a big and hearty breakfast.

# Donuts

**Prep time: 10 minutes**
**Cooking time: 15 minutes**

**Ingredients:**
- 3 cups self raising flour
- 1 1/2 cups white sugar
- 1 ½ cups brown sugar
- One cup full fat cream
- 1 cup butter
- One egg

**Directions:**
1. Preheat your Airfryer to 390 degrees F.
2. Combine the flour and butter using an electric hand mixer (ideally may also be done by hand).
3. Then add in the cream and egg. Mix on low.
4. To form donut shapes, use a cookie cutter (simple o shape) or a knife.
5. Use a bit of butter or coconut oil to grease an oven safe sheet or form. Place the donuts on the form.
6. Cook for 15 minutes. Repeat if more dough remains.
7. Top with powdered sugar, white sugar, chocolate frosting, sprinkles or whatever your heart desires.

# Zucchini Egg Breakfast frittata
**Prep time: 5 minutes**
**Cooking time: 15 minutes**

## Ingredients:
- Three zucchini, grated with a cheese grater
- One potato, grated
- One tablespoon parmesan
- Three eggs, beaten
- ½ cup milk (coconut milk, dairy milk or almond milk)
- One cup almond flour
- One teaspoon black pepper
- One teaspoon garlic powder
- ¼ teaspoon nutmeg
- One tablespoon olive oil

## Directions:
1. Preheat your Airfryer to 390 degrees F.
2. Combine the zucchini, potato, parmesan, eggs, milk almond flour and spices in a mixing bowl. Combine gently.
3. Place the olive oil on a heat safe dish.
4. Spoon out the zucchini mix and flatten to form patties.
5. Cook for 15 minutes.
6. Serve with sour cream, sliced tomatoes and toast for a healthy breakfast.

# Hash Browns

**Prep time: 5 minutes**
**Cooking time: 15 minutes**

**Ingredients:**
- One potato, grated
- Three eggs, beaten
- One cup whole grain flour
- One teaspoon black pepper
- One pinch salt
- One teaspoon garlic powder
- ¼ teaspoon nutmeg
- One tablespoon olive oil

**Directions:**
1. Preheat your Airfryer to 390 degrees F.
2. Combine the potato, eggs, flour and spices in a mixing bowl. Combine gently. (Stir by hand).
3. Place the olive oil on a heat safe dish.
4. Spoon out the potato mix and flatten to form patties.
5. Cook for 15 minutes.
6. Serve alongside eggs for a hearty breakfast.

# Vegetable Egg Pancake

**Prep time: 5 minutes**
**Cooking time: 15 minutes**
**Ingredients:**

- One zucchini, grated
- One beet, peeled and grated
- One carrot, grated
- One potato, grated
- One tablespoon parmesan
- Three eggs, beaten
- ½ cup milk (coconut milk, dairy milk or almond milk)
- One cup almond flour
- One teaspoon black pepper
- One teaspoon garlic powder
- One teaspoon onion powder
- ¼ teaspoon nutmeg
- One tablespoon olive oil

**Directions:**

1. Preheat your Airfryer to 390 degrees F.
2. Combine the zucchini, beet, carrot, potato, parmesan, eggs, milk almond flour and spices in a mixing bowl. Combine gently.
3. Place the olive oil on a heat safe dish.
4. Spoon out the vegetable mix and flatten to form patties.
5. Cook for 15 minutes.
6. Serve this colorful veggie pancake with sour cream, sliced tomatoes and toast for a healthy breakfast.

# Strawberry Vanilla Pancake

**Prep time: 5-10 minutes**
**Cooking time: 10 minutes**

## Ingredients:
- One cup rice flour
- One cup whole grain flour
- One teaspoon baking powder
- Three eggs
- 1 cup coconut milk
- One teaspoon vanilla powder (or vanilla extract)
- Two tablespoons maple syrup
- One cup coconut sugar (or brown sugar)
- ½ cup frozen and thawed strawberries

## Directions:
1. Preheat your Airfryer to 390 degrees F.
2. Mix the two types of flour, the baking powder, eggs, milk, vanilla, maple syrup and coconut sugar to a smooth consistency.
3. Then gently stir in the strawberries.
4. Grease a heat safe dish with butter or coconut oil.
5. Spread out some dough. Leave space between the pancakes. (Take turns to use up all the batter).
6. Cook for 10 minutes. Repeat if necessary.
7. Serve with maple syrup or cream.

# Wild Blueberry Chocolate Pancake

**Prep time: 5-10 minutes**
**Cooking time: 10 minutes**

## Ingredients:

- Two cups whole grain flour (spelt or wheat)
- One teaspoon baking powder
- Three eggs
- 1 cup almond milk
- One teaspoon cinnamon
- Two tablespoons cocoa powder
- Three tablespoons maple syrup
- One cup coconut sugar (or brown sugar)
- ½ cup frozen and thawed wild blueberries
- Optional: chocolate pieces

## Directions:

1. Preheat your Airfryer to 390 degrees F.
2. Mix the flour, the baking powder, eggs, milk, vanilla, maple syrup and coconut sugar to a smooth consistency.
3. Then gently stir in the blueberries (and the optional chocolate pieces).
4. Grease a heat safe dish with butter or coconut oil.
5. Spread out some dough. Leave space between the pancakes. (Take turns to use up all the batter).
6. Cook for 10 minutes. Repeat if necessary.
7. Serve with maple syrup or cream.

# Cranberry Cashew Muffins

**Prep time: 5-10 minutes**
**Cooking time: 15 minutes**

**Ingredients:**

- 1/2 corn flour (or corn starch)
- One cup whole grain flour
- One teaspoon baking powder
- Three eggs
- 1 cup coconut milk
- One tablespoon cashew nut butter
- One teaspoon vanilla powder (or vanilla extract)
- Two tablespoons maple syrup
- One cup coconut sugar (or brown sugar)
- ½ cup dried cranberries
- ½ cup cashews (whole or pieces)
- One pinch of sea salt

**Directions:**

1. Preheat your Airfryer to 390 degrees F.
2. Mix the two types of flour, the baking powder, eggs, milk, vanilla, maple syrup, pinch of salt and coconut sugar to a smooth consistency.
3. Fold in the cranberries and cashews.
4. Fill muffin cups with the batter.
5. Place in the Air fryer and cook for 15 minutes.
6. Serve with butter or as is for a yummy sit down breakfast or enjoy on the go.

# Cheesy Savory Airfryer Maffins

**Prep time: 5-10 minutes**
**Cooking time: 15 minutes**
**Ingredients:**

- 1/2 corn flour (or corn starch)
- One cup whole grain flour
- One teaspoon baking powder
- Three eggs
- 1 cup coconut milk
- One cup cream cheese
- ½ cup bacon pieces
- One pinch of sea salt
- One cup mozzarella cheese

**Directions:**

1. Preheat your Airfryer to 390 degrees F.
2. Combine all the ingredients in a large mixing bowl.
3. Stir by hand using a large wooden spoon ideally.
4. Fill muffin cups with the mixture.
5. Bake for 15 minutes.
6. Enjoy.

# Protein Breakfast

**Prep time: 5-10 minutes**
**Cooking time: 15 minutes**
**Ingredients:**

- One cup almond flour
- One teaspoon baking powder
- Three eggs
- 1 cup coconut milk
- One cup cream cheese
- Three tablespoons pea protein
- ½ cup chicken or turkey strips
- One pinch of sea salt
- One cup mozzarella cheese

**Directions:**

1. Preheat your Airfryer to 390 degrees F.
2. Combine all the ingredients in a large mixing bowl.
3. Stir by hand using a large wooden spoon ideally.
4. Fill muffin cups with the mixture.
5. Bake for 15 minutes.
6. Enjoy.

# Bacon Wrap

**Prep time: 5-10 minutes**
**Cooking time: 10 minutes**

## Ingredients:
- Three tortillas
- Six strips fried bacon
- Two scrambled eggs
- Three tablespoons cream cheese
- Three tablespoons salsa
- One cup pepper jack cheese

## Directions:
1. Preheat your Airfryer to 390 degrees F.
2. Spread the cream cheese onto the tortillas.
3. Divide the eggs evenly between the three tortillas.
4. Place two strips of bacon on each wrap.
5. Top with the cheese.
6. Roll up.
7. Fry in the Air fryer for 10 minutes.

---

# Cream Cheese Breakfast Puff

**Prep time: 5 minutes**
**Cooking time: 15 minutes**

## Ingredients:
- Three pre made pastry dough sheets
- Two cups cream cheese
- Three tablespoons strawberry jam
- One egg white, beaten

## Directions:
1. Preheat your Airfryer to 390 degrees F.
2. Spread the cream cheese onto the three pastry sheets.
3. Place one tablespoon of jam onto each pastry.
4. Pinch together the ends to form puffs. (Use a bit of egg brushed onto the edges to get the ends to stick.)
5. Place in the Airfryer on a greased heat safe dish.
6. Enjoy warm or save for later. Double up recipe for more people.

# Warm Chia Porridge for the Airfryer

**Prep time: 5-10 minutes**
**Cooking time: 5 minutes**

**Ingredients:**
- Two cups steel cut oats
- One cup chia seeds
- One tablespoon almond butter
- One tablespoon coconut oil
- Four cups coconut milk
- Four tablespoons maple syrup

**Directions:**
1. Preheat your Airfryer to 390 degrees F.
2. Mix together the ingredients smoothly.
3. Place in the Airfryer to warm for just five minutes.
4. Stir and serve. Top with berries or jam.

# Coconut breakfast muffin

**Prep time: 5-10 minutes**
**Cooking time: 10 minutes**
**Ingredients:**
- ½ cup coconut flour
- One cup whole grain flour
- One teaspoon baking powder
- Three eggs
- 1 cup coconut milk
- One teaspoon vanilla powder (or vanilla extract)
- Two tablespoons maple syrup
- One cup coconut sugar (or brown sugar)
- ½ cup shredded coconut
- One teaspoon coconut essence (natural)

**Directions:**
1. Preheat your Airfryer to 390 degrees F.
2. Mix all the ingredients together to form a smooth batter.
3. Pour the batter into muffin cups.
4. Place in the Airfryer and cook for 10 minutes.

# Raspberry Cream Cheese Breakfast Muffins

**Prep time: 5-10 minutes**
**Cooking time: 10 minutes**
**Ingredients:**

- ½ cup ground flaxseed
- One cup whole grain flour
- One teaspoon baking powder
- Three eggs
- 1 cup coconut milk
- One teaspoon vanilla powder (or vanilla extract)
- Two tablespoons maple syrup
- One cup coconut sugar (or brown sugar)
- One cup cream cheese
- One cup frozen and thawed raspberries

**Directions:**

1. Preheat your Airfryer to 390 degrees F.
2. Mix all the ingredients together to form a smooth batter.
3. Pour the batter into muffin cups.
4. Place in the Airfryer and cook for 10 minutes.
5. Enjoy.

# Lunch

## Luxury Grilled Cheese Sandwich

**Prep time: 7 minutes**
**Cooking time: 8 minutes**

Ingredients:
- 4 slices of rye bread
- One tablespoon butter
- 2 slices cheddar cheese
- 2 slices mozzarella cheese
- 2 slices havarti cheese
- 1/4 teaspoon black pepper
- 1 cup shredded carrots

Directions:
1. Preheat your air fryer to 390 degrees F.
2. Lightly coat each slice of bread with butter.
3. Top the slices of bread with the cheese and sprinkle with the pepper. Top with the carrots and place a slice of bread one on top of the other to form two sandwiches.
4. Place in the Fryer basket.
5. Cool in the Airfryer for 8 minutes or until the cheese is melted.

## Mushroom Melt Open "Sandwich" (gluten free, vegetarian)

**Prep time: 5 minutes**
**Cooking time: 8 minutes**

Ingredients:
- 4 portabella mushroom caps (stems removed)
- 4 tablespoons sour cream
- 1/4 teaspoon black pepper
- 1/4 teaspoon thyme
- 2 cups sharp cheddar cheese

Directions:
1. Preheat your air fryer to 390 degrees F.
2. Place a tablespoon of sour cream in each mushroom cap. Add the black pepper and thyme. Top with the cheese.
3. Place in the fryer basket and air fry for 8 minutes or until the cheese is completely melted.

# Stuffed Zucchini Deluxe
**Prep time: 5-8 minutes**
**Cooking time: 8 minutes**

**Ingredients:**
- 3 large zucchinis
- 1 cup shredded pepper jack cheese
- One tablespoon sour cream
- 3 tablespoons breadcrumbs
- One tablespoon bacon bits
- 1/4 teaspoon salt
- 1/4 teaspoon black pepper

**Directions:**
1. Preheat your air fryer to 390 degrees F.
2. Cut off the ends of the zucchini. Slice the zucchinis in half lengthwise to form "boats". Scoop out most of the "meat" from each zucchini boat. Save the zucchini "meat" and place in a bowl.
3. Add the remaining ingredients to the bowl with the zucchini "meat". Stir by hand to combine.
4. Spoon the contents of the bowl into each zucchini boat.
5. Place the stuffed zucchini in the fryer basket and put inside of the Airfryer. Cook for 8 minutes or until the cheese is fully melted.
6. Serve with a little side salad for a good lunch.

# Super Eggplant Stromboli
**Prep time: 10 minutes**
**Cooking time: 25 minutes**

## Ingredients:
- One egg, beaten
- One tablespoon butter
- One pizza crust (thawed if originally frozen)
- 2 cups mozzarella cheese
- 1 tsp dried or fresh basil
- One eggplant, cut into bits
- 1 1/2 cups pizza sauce
- One clove garlic, chopped

## Directions:
1. Preheat your air fryer to 390 degrees F.
2. Roll out the pizza crust.
3. Place the sauce, the cheese, basil, eggplant and garlic inside the crust.
4. Roll up the crust from one side to another.
5. Brush with the beaten egg.
6. Place in the fryer basket and fry for 25 minutes or until golden and crispy.

# Ultra Easy Extremely Delicious Pizza

**Prep time: 5 minutes**
**Cooking time: 14 minutes**

## Ingredients:
- 2 baguettes, sliced in half lengthwise and once again in the middle
- One cup tomato sauce (pizza sauce or pasta sauce of your choice)
- Two cups pepper jack or mozarella cheese (or your choice of cheese)
- Toppings (pepperoni, vegetables such as peppers, onions, etc)

## Directions:
1. Preheat your air fryer to 390 degrees F.
2. Spread tomato sauce onto the flat surface of each baguette half. Top with cheese and other toppings.
3. Place in the fryer basket.
4. Cook for 14 minutes until the cheese is melted and each baguette is nice and crispy.

# Chickpea veggie burgers

**Prep time: 10 minutes**
**Cooking time: 12-15 minutes**

## Ingredients:
- 1 can of chickpeas or 1.5 cups cooked chickpeas
- 1 tablespoon of chopped onion
- 1 teaspoon of dried or fresh chives
- 1 clove of chopped garlic
- 1 chopped yellow bell pepper
- A pinch of salt and pepper
- 1 tablespoon of olive oil

## Directions:
1. Preheat the Airfryer to 360 degrees F.
2. In a mixing bowl, combine the chickpeas with the chopped veggies and salt and pepper. Mash the mixture with a hand masher (or place in a food processor and pulse for 30 seconds).
3. Pick up a handful of the mixture and flatten it onto a piece of parchment paper. Drizzle with a little olive oil and put in the Airfryer in an oven safe form.
4. Bake for about 12 minutes.
5. Repeat the process until all of the chickpea mixture has been used (depending on how many veggie burgers you want to make.
6. Serve with veggie chips, salad and good bread.

# Black bean veggie burgers

**Prep time: 10 minutes**
**Cooking time: 12-15 minutes**

**Ingredients:**
- 1 can of black beans or 1.5 cups cooked black beans
- 1 tablespoon of chopped onion
- 1 teaspoon of dried or fresh chives
- 1 clove of chopped garlic
- 1 chopped yellow bell pepper
- A pinch of salt and pepper
- 1 tablespoon of olive oil

**Directions:**
1. Preheat the Airfryer to 360 degrees F.
2. In a mixing bowl, combine the black beans with the chopped veggies and salt and pepper. Mash the mixture with a hand masher (or place in a food processor and pulse for 30 seconds).
3. Pick up a handful of the mixture and flatten it onto a piece of parchment paper. Drizzle with a little olive oil and put in the Airfryer in an oven safe form.
4. Bake for about 12 minutes.
5. Repeat the process until all of the black bean mixture has been used (depending on how many veggie burgers you want to make.
6. Serve with veggie chips, salad and good bread. Guacamole is the perfect condiment with black bean burgers for a delicious, Mexican inspired vegetarian meal.

# Turkey Rolls

**Prep time: 5 minutes**
**Cooking time: 10 minutes**

## Ingredients:

- 4 slices turkey breast (cold cuts can be used, but best taste is achieved with sliced turkey breast)
- One cup sliced fresh mozzarella
- One tomato, sliced
- 1/2 cup fresh basil
- 4 chive shoots (for tying the rolls)

## Directions:

1. Preheat your air fryer to 390 degrees F.
2. Place slices of mozzarella, tomato and basil onto each turkey slice. Roll up and tie with a chive shoot (looks like a blade of grass but tastes so much better)
3. Place in the Air fryer and cook for 10 minutes. Serve with a side salad.

# Spicy Stuffed Peppers (low carb, gluten free)

**Prep time: 8 minutes**
**Cooking time: 12 minutes**

## Ingredients:

- 4 red peppers, with the tops sliced off and the inner contents removed
- 2 minced meat, fried
- 3 cups sour cream
- 1 teaspoon garlic powder
- 1/4 teaspoon pepper
- 2 cups shredded cheddar cheese

## Directions:

1. Preheat your air fryer to 390 degrees F.
2. Combine the browned and fried meat with the sour cream in a bowl. Add the garlic and pepper and hand mix with a large spoon.
3. Spoon the meat mixture into each pepper. Top with the shredded cheese.
4. Place in the Airfryer basket and cook for 12 minutes or until the cheese is melted.

# Crispy Carrot Noodles (Gluten free, low carb)
**Prep time: 5 minutes**
**Cooking time: 10 minutes**

## Ingredients:
- 7 large carrots, made into noodles with a spiralizer or mandolin
- One tablespoon olive oil
- 1/4 teaspoon black pepper
- 1/2 teaspoon garlic powder
- Two tablespoons sour cream
- Two tablespoons bacon bits

## Directions:
1. Preheat your air fryer to 390 degrees F.
2. Put the carrot "noodles" into a mixing bowl with the olive oil, sea salt, pepper and garlic powder. Stir with a spoon or use your hands to distribute the oil and spices.
3. Place in the Air fryer basket. Cook for 10 minutes or until nice and crispy.
4. Remove from the Air fryer. Top with sour cream and bacon bits.
5. Enjoy!

# Zucchini Roll Ups (low carb, gluten free, vegetarian)
**Prep time: 5 minutes**
**Cooking time: 5 minutes**

## Ingredients:
- 3 zucchinis, sliced thinly lengthwise (with a mandolin or very good knife)
- One tablespoon olive oil
- One cup goat cheese
- 1/4 teaspoon black pepper

## Directions:
1. Preheat your air fryer to 390 degrees F.
2. Brush each zucchini strip with a bit of olive oil (use a food brush)
3. Mix the sea salt and black pepper with the goat cheese.
4. Spoon a bit of goat cheese into the middle of each strip of zucchini.
5. Roll up each zucchini and fasten with a toothpick.
6. Place in the Airfryer and cook for five minutes. The cheese will be warm and the zucchini slightly crispy.
7. Top with tomato sauce or enjoy as is for a light lunch or snack.

# Baked Stuffed Alfredo Potato (vegetarian, gluten free)

**Prep time: 5 minutes**
**Cooking time: 16 minutes**

**Ingredients:**
- 3 large potatoes (skin intact)
- One cup of your favorite alfredo sauce
- One cup of mozzarella cheese
- 1 teaspoon red pepper
- 1 teaspoon garlic powder

**Directions:**
1. Preheat your air fryer to 390 degrees F.
2. Cut just a slit in each potato lengthwise. Place them in the Air fryer basket for 10 minutes.
3. Remove the potatoes. Spoon out about 80% of the contents of each potato and place in a bowl.
4. Add the alfredo sauce, mozzarella cheese, pepper, salt and garlic powder. Combine with an electric mixer or by hand.
5. Stuff each potato with the cheesy potato mixture.
6. Put back in the Air fryer and cook for 6-8 more minutes.

# Cheesy Mushroom Caps

**Prep time: 5-10 minutes**
**Cooking time: 10 minutes**

**Ingredients:**
- 4 portabella mushroom caps
- 2 cups cream cheese
- One tablespoon garlic powder
- 1 cup mozzarella cheese

**Directions:**
1. Preheat your Airfryer to 390 degrees F.
2. Mix together the garlic powder and cream cheese in a medium sized mixing bowl.
3. Spread onto each mushroom.
4. Top with mozzarella cheese.
5. Place in the Airfryer and cook for 10 minutes.

# Mushroom Cordon Bleu

**Prep time: 5-10 minutes**
**Cooking time: 10 minutes**

## Ingredients:
- 4 portabella mushroom caps
- 2 cups cream cheese
- One egg
- One tablespoon garlic powder
- One tablespoon onion powder
- 1 cup mozzarella cheese
- 4 slices ham (boiled ham sliced, or cold cuts)
- One egg beaten
- Two cups chickpea flour

## Directions:
1. Preheat your Airfryer to 390 degrees F.
2. Mix together the garlic powder, one egg, onion powder and cream cheese in a medium sized mixing bowl.
3. Spread onto each mushroom.
4. Top with mozzarella cheese and a slice of ham.
5. Dip each mushroom in the egg, and then in the bowl containing the chickpea flour.
6. Place in the Airfryer and cook for 10 minutes.

# Stuffed Tomatoes (vegan and non vegan variation)

**Prep time: 5-10 minutes**
**Cooking time: 7 minutes**

## Ingredients:
- 4 large "beefsteak" tomatoes
- One cup sunflower seed butter
- One cup vegan shredded cheese (or dairy cheese)
- One tablespoon garlic powder
- One tablespoon onion powder
- ½ cup baby spinach
- ½ teaspoon dried basil

## Directions:
1. Preheat your Airfryer to 390 degrees F.
2. Slice the tops off of the tomatoes and scoop out most of the insides.
3. Mix together the vegan cheese, sunflower seed butter, garlic powder, onion powder, spinach and basil.
4. Scoop into each tomato.

5. Place each tomato in the Air fryer and cook for 7 minutes.

# Filled Spinach leaves
**Prep time: 5 minutes**
**Cooking time: 5 minutes**

**Ingredients:**
- 8 large leaves of spinach
- 1 ½ cup cream cheese
- One tablespoon garlic powder
- ¼ teaspoon chives
- 4 strips of bacon, chopped into bits

**Directions:**
1. Preheat your Airfryer to 390 degrees F.
2. Mix together the cream cheese, garlic powder, chives and bacon bits.
3. Scoop a bit of the cheese mixture into the spinach leaves.
4. Fry quickly for 4-5 minutes.
5. Serve with salad for a light lunch.

# Spinach Feta Pastry
**Prep time: 5 minutes**
**Cooking time: 14 minutes**

**Ingredients:**
- 4 sheets of flaky pastry dough (filo works well)
- 2 cups frozen and thawed spinach
- 2 cloves garlic, chopped finely
- 2 tablespoons olive oil
- One cup feta cheese, crumbled
- One egg, beaten

**Directions:**
1. Preheat your Airfryer to 390 degrees F.
2. In a medium sized mixing bowl, combine the spinach, garlic, cheese, and one tablespoon of olive oil.
3. Spoon some of the mixture onto each pastry. Fold and tuck in the ends. Brush with the egg to make the ends stick.
4. Brus the tops of each pastry with olive oil.
5. Cut small slits into each pastry.
6. Air fry for 14 minutes.
7. Serve with salad and tzaziki.

# Fried Sweet Potato Pumpkin noodles

**Prep time: 5 minutes**
**Cooking time: 10 minutes**

## Ingredients:

- 3 large sweet potatoes, peeled and spiralized into noodle shapes with a mandolin or noodle spiralizer
- One cup pumpkin puree (pre cooked pumpkin chunks or pumpkin puree)
- ½ cup coconut cream
- 2 cloves garlic, chopped
- One teaspoon black pepper

## Directions:

1. Preheat your Airfryer to 390 degrees F.
2. Stir up the pumpkin puree with coconut cream, garlic and black pepper.
3. Add the sweet potato "noodles".
4. Place in a heat safe dish and then in the Air fryer.
5. Fry for 10 minutes.
6. Optionally top with shredded mozzarella. Enjoy!

# Fried Rosemary Carrot noodles

**Prep time: 5 minutes**
**Cooking time: 10 minutes**

## Ingredients:

- 4 large carrots, peeled and spiralized into noodle shapes with a mandolin or noodle spiralizer
- One tablespoon olive oil
- One teaspoon dried or fresh rosemary
- One pinch sea salt

## Directions:

1. Preheat your Airfryer to 390 degrees F.
2. Toss your carrot noodles in a mixing bowl with the olive oil, rosemary and salt. Use your hands to distribute the oil evenly, if needed.
3. Place in a heat safe dish and then in the Air fryer.
4. Fry for 10 minutes.
5. Top with sour cream, bacon or chicken if so desired for an extra delicious (low carb) lunch.

# Fried Cabbage Patties

**Prep time: 5 minutes**
**Cooking time: 10 minutes**

**Ingredients:**
- Two cups shredded purple cabbage
- Four eggs, beaten
- One cup cornmeal
- One pinch sea salt
- One tablespoon onion powder
- One teaspoon black pepper
- One tablespoon olive oil

**Directions:**
1. Preheat your Airfryer to 390 degrees F.
2. Combine all of the ingredients except the olive oil in a mixing bowl.
3. Grease a heat safe dish using the olive oil.
4. Spoon the mixture onto the dish and form patties but pushing down with a spoon.
5. Cook for 15 minutes.
6. Serve with bread as a vegetarian burger, or with salad as a vegetable based light meal.

# Broccoli Bacon Burger

**Prep time: 5 minutes**
**Cooking time: 12 minutes**

**Ingredients:**
- One cup broccoli florets, cooked lightly
- One cup potato meal
- Three eggs, beaten
- One cup bacon bits (freshly fried bacon cut into bits)
- One tablespoon black pepper
- One tablespoon olive oil

**Directions:**
1. Preheat your Airfryer to 390 degrees F.
2. Combine all of the ingredients except the olive oil in a mixing bowl.
3. Grease a heat safe dish using the olive oil.
4. Spoon the mixture onto the dish and form patties but pushing down with a spoon.
5. Cook for 12 minutes.
6. Enjoy.

# Buckwheat Ham and Cheese Balls

**Prep time: 5 minutes**
**Cooking time: 15 minutes**

## Ingredients:
- Two cups buckwheat flour
- One cup cooked ham, cut into cubes
- One cup cheddar cheese, shredded
- Three eggs, beaten
- One tablespoon black pepper
- One teaspoon onion powder
- ¼ teaspoon nutmeg powder
- Two tablespoons olive oil

## Directions:
1. Preheat your Airfryer to 390 degrees F.
2. Combine all of the ingredients except the olive oil in a mixing bowl.
3. Grease a heat safe dish using the olive oil.
4. Spoon the mixture onto the dish and form balls using your hands.
5. Cook for 15 minutes.
6. Serve with bread as a vegetarian burger, or with salad as a vegetable based light meal.

# Millet Beef Burger

**Prep time: 5 minutes**
**Cooking time: 15 minutes**

## Ingredients:
- One cup millet flour
- Two cups ground beef
- Three eggs
- One teaspoon black pepper
- One teaspoon thyme
- One tablespoon garlic powder

## Directions:
1. Preheat your Airfryer to 390 degrees F.
2. Combine all of the ingredients except the olive oil in a mixing bowl.
3. Grease a heat safe dish using the olive oil.
4. Spoon the mixture onto the dish and form patties but pushing down with a spoon.
5. Cook for 15 minutes.

# Chickpea Pork Patties

**Prep time: 5 minutes**
**Cooking time: 20 minutes**

**Ingredients:**
- Three pork filets
- One cup chickpea flour
- One tablespoon garlic powder
- One tablespoon black pepper
- One tablespoon paprika powder
- One egg, beaten
- One tablespoon olive oil

**Directions:**
1. Preheat your Airfryer to 390 degrees F.
2. Mix the dry ingredients (flour, garlic, pepper, paprika) in a large mixing bowl.
3. Dip each filet first in the egg and then in the flour combination.
4. Grease a heat safe dish with the olive oil.
5. Place the filets on the dish and cook for 20 minutes.
6. Serve alongside a salad with dipping sauce and/or dressing.

# Turkey Bacon Bean burger

**Prep time: 5 minutes**
**Cooking time: 20 minutes**

**Ingredients:**
- One cup black beans, cooked and mashed in a food processor
- 4 eggs, beaten
- One cup turkey bacon, cut up into bits
- One cup ground turkey
- One tablespoon black pepper
- One pinch sea salt
- One tablespoon olive oil

**Directions:**
1. Preheat your Airfryer to 390 degrees F.
2. Combine all of the ingredients except the olive oil in a mixing bowl.
3. Grease a heat safe dish.
4. Spoon the mixture onto the dish and form patties but pushing down with a spoon.
5. Cook for 20 minutes.

# Zucchini Bacon Lasagne

**Prep time: 5-10 minutes**
**Cooking time: 20 minutes**

## Ingredients:
- Two zucchini, sliced thinly lengthwise using a mandolin
- 6 strips bacon
- Two cups ricotta cheese
- Two cups mozzarella cheese
- One tablespoon garlic powder
- Two tablespoons olive oil

## Directions:
1. Preheat your Airfryer to 390 degrees F.
2. Grease a lasagne pan with olive oil.
3. Combine the garlic powder and ricotta cheese.
4. Layer on the zucchini to the pan. Then the ricotta. Then add the bacon. Follow by some mozzarella cheese.
5. Repeat by adding zucchini, ricotta and then mozzarella.
6. Place in the Air fryer and cook for 20 minutes.
7. Enjoy!

# Turkey Stuffed Peppers

**Prep time: 5 minutes**
**Cooking time: 25 minutes**

## Ingredients:
- Three red bell peppers, with the tops sliced off and all seeds removed
- One cup cooked turkey, cut into strips
- ½ cup turkey bacon, cut into bits
- One cup cream cheese
- One cup pepper jack cheese
- One tablespoon black pepper
- One tablespoon olive oil

## Directions:
1. Preheat your Airfryer to 390 degrees F.
2. Combine the turkey, bacon, cream cheese and pepper in a mixing bowl.
3. Grease a heat safe dish.
4. Spoon the turkey and bacon mixture into each bell pepper.
5. Top with shredded pepper jack cheese.
6. Cook for 25 minutes.
7. Enjoy.

# Stuffed Pizza Pastries

**Prep time: 5 minutes**
**Cooking time: 18 minutes**

**Ingredients:**
- 4 sheets of flaky pastry dough (filo works well)
- One cup tomato (pizza) sauce
- 1 ½ cups cheese
- One clove garlic, chopped
- One tablespoon parmesan cheese
- Pepperoni (optional)
- One egg, beaten
- One tablespoon olive oil

**Directions:**
1. Preheat your Airfryer to 390 degrees F.
2. Spread the pizza sauce on each sheet.
3. Then top with the cheese, garlic and pepperoni.
4. Roll up and tuck in ends. Brush with egg.
5. Brush with olive oil on all sides.
6. Place on heat safe dish and cook for 18 minutes.

# Side dishes

## Sweet potato fries
**Prep time: 10 minutes**
**Cooking time: 12-15 minutes**

**Ingredients:**
- 3 large sweet potatoes, peeled
- 1 tablespoon of olive oil
- A pinch of sea salt

**Directions:**
1. Preheat the Airfryer to 390 degrees F.
2. Cut the sweet potatoes into quarters. Then cut them lengthwise to form fries.
3. In a bowl, combine the uncooked sweet potato fries with the tablespoon of olive oil and the pinch of sea salt. Make sure all of the fries are lightly coated with oil and salt.
4. Place the sweet potato pieces into the Airfryer basket. Cook for 12 minutes. Check when the 15 minutes have passed. Cook for an additional 2-3 minutes if the desired level of crispiness has not yet been achieved.
5. If your taste calls for more salt, add a bit more.
6. Enjoy with ketchup or any other type of condiment of your choice (sour cream and herbs, dressing, etc).

## Rosemary potatoes
**Prep time: 5 minutes**
**Cooking time: 12-15 minutes**

**Ingredients:**
- Three large white or red potatoes, cubed but not peeled
- 1 tablespoon of olive oil
- A pinch of sea salt
- 1/2 teaspoon of fresh or dried rosemary

**Directions:**
1. Preheat the Airfryer to 390 degrees F.
2. Combine the potatoes with the olive oil, the salt and the rosemary in a medium sized mixing bowl. Make sure the potatoes are evenly coated. A dash or two of additional olive oil may be used if desired.
3. Place the potatoes in the Airfryer basket. Cook for 12 minutes. Then check. If additional crispiness is wished, cook the potatoes for 2-3 more minutes.
4. Serve with sour cream.

# Crispy kale

**Prep time: 5 minutes**
**Cooking time: 8 minutes**

**Ingredients**:
- 4 handfuls of kale, washed and pulled from the stems
- 1 tablespoon of olive oil
- A pinch of sea salt

**Directions:**
1. Preheat the Airfryer to 360 degrees F.
2. Combine the kale with the olive oil and the salt in a mixing bowl. Make sure all of the leaves are coated.
3. Place the kale in the Airfryer basket and cook for 8 minutes. Remove and serve with your favorite main meals.

# Spicy crispy cabbage

**Prep time: 5 minutes**
**Cooking time: 10 minutes**

**Ingredients**
- A half a head of white cabbage, chopped into small pieces and washed
- 1 tablespoon of coconut oil, melted to liquid
- A pinch of sea salt
- A pinch of chili, cayenne pepper, garlic powder

**Directions:**
1. Preheat the Airfryer to 390 degrees F.
2. In a large mixing bowl, combine the chopped cabbage with the coconut oil and the spices. Take care that the cabbage is lightly coated.
3. Place the cabbage in the Airfryer basket. Fry for 10 minutes.
4. Enjoy!

# Hasselback Potatoes

**Prep time:** 15 minutes
**Cooking time:** 40 minutes

## Ingredients:
- 18 medium potatoes
- 5 tbsp olive oil
- 1.6 oz butter
- pepper
- salt

## Directions:
1. Preheat your air fryer to 390 degrees F.
2. Cut potatoes thinly lengthwise.
3. Lightly coat potatoes with oil and butter.
4. Add pepper and salt to taste.
5. Put it in the airfryer for 40 minutes.

# Garlic Potatoes

**Prep time:** 10 minutes
**Cooking time:** 15 minutes

## Ingredients:
- 3 russet baking potatoes
- 1-2 tbsp olive oil
- 1 tbsp salt
- 1 tbsp garlic

## Directions:
1. Preheat your air fryer to 390 degrees F.
2. Create holes in the potatoes using a fork.
3. Sprinkle them with the oil and salt.
4. Rub garlic evenly on the potatoes.
5. Put potatoes into the air fryer basket.
6. Bake for 35-40 minutes.
7. Also you could top it with parsley for example

# Curry zucchini
**Prep time: 5 minutes**
**Cooking time: 8-10 minutes**

**Ingredients:**
- 2 washed, sliced zucchinis (sliced to form "coins")
- 1 tablespoon of olive oil
- 1 pinch of sea salt
- Curry mix (try turmeric, chili, black pepper, fenugreek)

**Directions:**
1. Preheat the Airfryer to 390 degrees F.
2. In a large bowl, combine the zucchini slices, the oil, salt and spices.
3. Place the zucchini "coins" in the Airfryer basket and cook for 8-10 minutes.
4. Serve with sour cream alongside your favorite main dishes.

# Vegetable medley
**Prep time: 5 minutes**
**Cooking time: 4 minutes**

**Ingredients:**
- Broccoli (cut into bite-sized pieces),
- Carrots (sliced into bite sized pieces),
- Red bell pepper (cut into bite-sized bits),
- Cauliflower bits,
- Corn,
- Green bean bits
- A pinch of sea salt

**Directions:**
1. Preheat Airfryer to 360 degrees F.
2. Put the vegetables into the Airfryer basket. Cook for 4 minutes. (The point is to get the veggies warm, not to actually fry them to a crisp.)
3. Sprinkle with salt. Enjoy as part of your healthy, low-calorie dinner.

# Roast Vegetables

**Prep time: 10 minutes**
**Cooking time: 20 minutes**

## Ingredients:
- 7 oz peeled parsnips
- 7 oz peeled celeriac
- 7 oz pumpkin without seeds
- 1 red onion
- 1 tbsp fresh thyme
- 1 tbsp olive oil
- sea salt
- ground black pepper

## Directions:
1. Preheat your air fryer to 390 degrees F.
2. Lightly grease round baking dish (about 6 inches diameter).
3. Cut celeriac, pumpkin and parsnip into cubes.
4. Add in 1 egg and apricot jam. Mix it.
5. Combine vegetables with onion, thyme, salt, oil and pepper. Stir thoroughly.
6. Put the mixture into air fryer basket.
7. Cook for 18-20 minutes until brown.

# Stuffed Potatoes

**Prep time: 15 minutes**
**Cooking time: 35 minutes**

## Ingredients:

- 4 large potatoes (peeled)
- olive oil
- 2 bacon (rashers)
- 1/2 brown onion
- 1/4 cup grated cheese

## Directions:

1. Preheat your air fryer to 350 degrees F.
2. Cut potatoes in half.
3. Lightly brush the potatoes with the oil.
4. Put in air fryer basket and cook for 10 minutes.
5. Brush potatoes again with the oil and cook for another 10 minutes.
6. Brush again and cook for another 10 minutes.
7. Make a hole in the baked potato halves for stuffing.
8. Lightly saute the bacon and onion in a frying pan over medium heat. Add cheese and stir through. Remove from the heat.
9. Stuff the potatoes with mixture.
10. Cook in airfryer for additional 4-5 minutes.

# Four cheese pizza

**Prep time: 10 minutes**
**Cooking time: 12 minutes (x 4-6 for each pizza)**

**Ingredients:**
- 1 large pizza crust, divided into 4-6 smaller rounds
- Red pizza sauce of your choice (or try a layer of sour cream with sliced tomatoes)
- Four cheese shredded blend

**Directions:**
1. Preheat the airfryer to 390 degrees F.
2. Put one of the pizza crust rounds into an oven safe dish. Top with sauce and then cheese.
3. Place in the Airfryer and cook for 12 minutes.
4. Repeat the process until all of the mini pizzas have been baked in the Airfryer.

# Vegetarian, gluten free lasagna

**Prep time: 10 minutes**
**Cooking time: 10 minutes**

**Ingredients:**
- 3 zucchinis
- 1 eggplant
- 1 cup of shredded carrots
- 1 cup of spinach
- 2 cups of mozzarella cheese
- 1 glass of your choice of tomato sauce
- 1 cup of ricotta cheese
- 3 tablespoons of olive oil

**Directions:**
1. Preheat the Airfryer to 360 degrees F.
2. Cut the zucchini and eggplant into as thin of strips as possible using a mandolin.
3. Drizzle a little olive oil into the bottom of an oven safe dish.
4. Place a layer of zucchini strips. Add a little tomato sauce, and a little ricotta cheese. Then form a layer of mozzarella. Top with a layer of eggplant. Add more sauce, then a few leaves of spinach, then more cheese.
5. Next, add another layer of zucchini, followed by sauce, then the carrots and then more cheese.
6. Continue this way until all of the vegetables have been used.
7. End with a topping of sauce and finally cheese.
8. Put the form in the Airfryer and cook for 10 minutes.
9. Remove and enjoy with bread and salad.

# Broccoli and cheese

**Prep time: 5 minutes**
**Cooking time: 9 minutes**

Ingredients:
- One whole head of broccoli, washed and cut into bite-sized bits
- A pinch of sea salt
- One tablespoon of olive oil
- Sharp cheddar cheese

**Directions:**
1. Preheat the Airfryer to 360 degrees F.
2. Combine the broccoli pieces in a medium sized mixing bowl along with the sea salt and olive oil.
3. Place the broccoli in the Airfryer basket. Cook for 6 minutes.
4. Take the basket out and top the broccoli with cheese. Cook for 3 more minutes.
5. Serve the delicious broccoli with chicken, sour cream, and rosemary potatoes.

# Roasted Carrots

**Prep time: 5 minutes**
**Cooking time: 35 minutes**

Ingredients:
- 4 cups carrot chunks
- 1 tsp herbes de provence
- 2 tsp olive oil
- 4 tbsp orange juice

**Directions:**
1. Preheat your air fryer to 320 degrees F.
2. In a bowl combine carrot chunks, oil and herbes.
3. Cook for 25-28 minutes.
4. Take out of airfryer and dip in a bowl with orange juice.
5. Return to air fryer and roast for additional 7 minutes.

# Cauliflower

**Prep time: 10 minutes**
**Cooking time: 20 minutes**

## Ingredients:
- 1 cauliflower (small head)
- 1 cup flour
- 1/2 cup cornstarch
- 1 tsp baking powder
- 1/2 tsp salt
- 1 cup water
- 1 tbsp hot sauce
- 2 cups seasoned breadcrumbs
- olive oil

## Directions:
1. Preheat your air fryer to 365 degrees F.
2. In a bowl, combine flour, cornstarch, salt and baking powder.
3. Add sauce and water. Stir batter until smooth.
4. Cut cauliflower into small pieces.
5. Dip each cauliflower piece in the batter and then into breadcrumbs.
6. Put cauliflower in air fryer basket.
7. Cook for 17-20 minutes.

# Broccoli

**Prep time: 10 minutes**
**Cooking time: 25 minutes**

**Ingredients:**
- 2 pounds broccoli
- 2 tbsp olive oil
- 1 tsp salt
- 1/2 tsp ground black pepper
- ⅓ cup olives (pitted)
- 2 tsp grated lemon zest
- 1/4 cup Parmesan cheese (sliced)
- 6 cups water

**Directions:**
1. Preheat your air fryer to 390 degrees F.
2. Stem and cut broccoli into 1-11/2-inch florets.
3. Pour 6 cups of water into saucepan and boil it.
4. Add broccoli to the water and cook 3-5 minutes.
5. Take broccoli out of the water and stir with oil, pepper & salt.
6. Put broccoli in air fryer basket.
7. Cook for 13-15 minutes.
8. Take broccoli out of the airfryer and add lemon zest, olives and cheese to taste.

# Garlic bread

**Prep time: 5 minutes**
**Cooking time: 10 minutes**

**Ingredients:**
- A baguette cut into thin bread sticks
- 1 tablespoon of butter
- 1/2 teaspoon Garlic powder
- A bit of chives

**Directions:**
1. Preheat the Airfryer to 390 degrees F.
2. Spread the butter onto the bread sticks. Sprinkle evenly with garlic powder.
3. Top with the chives.
4. Place the breadsticks face up in the Airfryer. Cook for 8 minutes. Remove and enjoy with your favorite pasta dish, or as a snack.

# Crispy cauliflower

**Prep time: 5 minutes**
**Cooking time: 10 minutes**

## Ingredients:

- 1 head of cauliflower, cut into bite-sized pieces
- 1 tablespoon of olive oil
- 1/2 teaspoon of sea salt
- A pinch of turmeric, chili and black pepper

## Directions:

1. Preheat the Airfryer to 360 degrees F.
2. Combine the cauliflower bits in a bowl with the olive oil, sea salt and spices. Coat evenly.
3. Place the cauliflower in the Airfryer basket. Cook for 10 minutes.
4. Serve with coconut cream or sour cream alongside your favorite main dishes.

# Rice

**Prep time: 10 minutes**
**Cooking time: 19 minutes**

## Ingredients:

- 2 pax overnight cooked rice
- 1 tbsp melted butter
- 4 garlic cloves
- 3 tbsp broccoli
- 2 tbsp carrot cubes
- 1 veal sausage
- 8-10 tbsp of creamy sauce
- 3 tbsp cheddar cheese
- 2 tbsp mozzarella cheese

## Directions:

1. Preheat your air fryer to 350 degrees F.
2. Mince garlic cloves and sauté for 1-2 minutes.
3. Add in broccoli florets, carrot and butter. Fry for 3-4 minutes.
4. Slice sausage and add to broccoli. Fry for 2-3 minutes
5. Add in the rice. Mix well.
6. Pour creamy sauce and stir well.
7. Shred cheddar and mozzarella cheese and sprinkle evenly.
8. Air fry for 8-10 minutes.

# Carrot fries

**Prep time: 5 minutes**
**Cooking time: 12-15 minutes**

**Ingredients:**
- 5 large carrots
- One tablespoon of olive oil
- 1/2 teaspoon of sea salt

**Directions:**
1. Preheat the Airfryer to 390 degrees F.
2. Wash and peel the carrots. Cut them lengthwise to form fries.
3. Combine the carrot sticks with the sea salt and olive oil in a mixing bowl. Coat evenly.
4. Place the carrot fries in the Airfryer basket. Cook for 12 minutes. If additional crispiness is desired, cook for another 2-3 minutes, checking periodically.
5. Serve with ketchup or sour cream alongside your favorite main dishes.

# Crispy Tofu

**Prep time: 10 minutes**
**Cooking time: 20 minutes**

**Ingredients:**
- 12 oz tofu
- 1 tsp sesame oil
- 1 tsp Maggi sauce
- 2 tbsp fish sauce
- 2 tbsp soy sauce
- 1 tsp goose fat

**Directions:**
1. Preheat your air fryer to 350 degrees F.
2. Chop tofu into 1 inch cubes.
3. In a bowl make a marinade - mix oil, Maggi sauce, fish and soy sauce.
4. Melt goose fat in microwave.
5. Pour the marinade into the bowl with tofu. Stir it.
6. Set aside for 30 minutes. Stir it a few times.
7. Put tofu in air fryer basket.
8. Cook for 8-10 minutes.
9. Turn tofu or shake it.
10. Cook for additional 8-10 minutes

# Ginger Cauliflower Bites

**Prep time: 5 minutes**
**Cooking time: 12 minutes**

**Ingredients:**
- One head cauliflower
- One egg, beaten
- One inch of ginger root, peeled and chopped
- One tablespoon ginger powder
- One tablespoon coconut oil for greasing pan

**Directions:**
1. Preheat your Airfryer to 390 degrees F.
2. Combine the egg and ginger.
3. Cut the cauliflower into florets.
4. Put the cauliflower into the bowl with the egg and ginger. Coat all pieces.
5. Place in a greased, oven safe dish.
6. Cook for 12 minutes.

# Broccoli Egg Rolls

**Prep time: 5 minutes**
**Cooking time: 10 minutes**

**Ingredients:**
- 4 sheets of rice "paper" (egg roll sheets)
- two eggs, beaten
- One cup broccoli florets
- One cup shredded carrots
- Two garlic cloves, finely chopped
- One tablespoon of coconut oil to grease the pan

**Directions:**
1. Preheat your Airfryer to 390 degrees F.
2. Mix the broccoli, carrots and garlic in a bowl.
3. Dip each piece of rice paper quickly into lukewarm water and remove immediately.
4. Distribute the veggie mix between the four pieces of rice paper.
5. Fold up each egg roll.
6. Dip in the egg mixture and place on a heat safe pan.
7. Cook for 10 minutes.
8. Serve with sweet and sour sauce or your choice of sauce.

# Cheese Egg Rolls

**Prep time: 5 minutes**
**Cooking time: 10 minutes**

## Ingredients:
- 4 sheets of rice "paper" (egg roll sheets)
- two eggs, beaten
- One onion, finely chopped
- 1 ½ cups cream cheese
- One cup swiss cheese, shredded
- One carrot, grated
- One tablespoon coconut oil for greasing pan

## Directions:
1. Preheat your Airfryer to 390 degrees F.
2. Mix the cheese, onion and carrot.
3. Dip each rice "paper" in lukewarm water and remove quickly. Spread flat on a clean surface.
4. Distribute the cheese mix among the rice sheets.
5. Wrap up and fold over the rice rolls.
6. Dip in the egg mix.
7. Place on a greased, heat safe form and cook in the Air fryer for 10 minutes.
8. Serve with sweet and sour sauce.

# Breaded Carrot Sticks

**Prep time: 5 minutes**
**Cooking time: 10 minutes**

## Ingredients:
- 5 large carrots cut into sticks
- One egg, beaten
- One cup chickpea flour
- One tablespoon black pepper
- One tablespoon garlic powder

## Directions:
1. Preheat your Airfryer to 390 degrees F.
2. Combine the chickpea, black pepper and garlic powder in a bowl.
3. Dip the carrots first into egg and then into the chickpea flour.
4. Place on a greased (with coconut oil or olive oi) oven safe dish.
5. Cook for 15 minutes.
6. Serve with sour cream.

# Peas and Cheese Rolls

**Prep time: 5 minutes**
**Cooking time: 10 minutes**

## Ingredients:
- 4 sheets of rice "paper" (egg roll sheets)
- two eggs, beaten
- One tablespoon onion powder
- One tablespoon garlic powder
- 1 cup cream cheese
- One cup cheddar cheese, shredded
- ½ cup peas, frozen and thawed
- ¼ cubed potatoes (cubed very small, to be about the size of the peas)
- One tablespoon coconut oil for greasing pan

## Directions:
1. Preheat your Airfryer to 390 degrees F.
2. Mix the cheese, peas, potatoes and the onion and garlic powder.
3. Dip each rice "paper" in lukewarm water and remove quickly. Spread flat on a clean surface.
4. Distribute the cheese mix among the rice sheets.
5. Wrap up and fold over the rice rolls.
6. Dip in the egg mix.
7. Place on a greased, heat safe form and cook in the Air fryer for 10 minutes.
8. Serve with sweet and sour sauce or chutney and sour cream as a side or as a snack or small meal.

# Tomato Pepper Bites

**Prep time: 5 minutes**
**Cooking time: 10 minutes**

## Ingredients:
- One cup sun dried tomatoes, soaked and chopped
- 3 peppers, quartered into "boat" shapes
- One tomato, chopped
- Two cloves garlic, chopped
- Two cups pepper jack cheese
- One tablespoon coconut oil for greasing pan

## Directions:
1. Preheat your Airfryer to 390 degrees F.
2. In a mixing bowl, combine the sun dried tomatoes, chopped tomato, garlic and cheese.
3. Spoon an even amount onto each pepper boat.
4. Place on a greased, heat safe dish.

5. Put in the Air fryer and cook for 10 minutes.

# Spicy Cheese Fried Chickpeas

**Prep time: 5 minutes**
**Cooking time: 10 minutes**

## Ingredients:
- Two cups chickpeas
- Two cups shredded pepper jack cheese
- One cup cream cheese
- Two tablespoons garlic powder
- One tablespoon chili powder

## Directions:
1. Preheat your Airfryer to 375 degrees F.
2. Combine the cream cheese with garlic and chili powder.
3. In a mixing bowl, combine the chickpeas and cream cheese.
4. Form the chickpea and cream cheese into balls.
5. Place the pepper jack cheese in a mixing bowl.
6. Roll the chickpea balls in the pepper jack cheese. Press so that the shredded cheese sticks.
7. Grease a heat safe pan with coconut oil.
8. Place in the Air fryer and cook for 10 minutes.
9. Serve with a tomato sauce as dip.

# Bacon Rice

**Prep time: 5 minutes**
**Cooking time: 15 minutes**

## Ingredients:
- Two cups cooked rice
- ½ cup crispy bacon
- One egg, beaten
- One tablespoon garlic powder
- One tablespoon black pepper
- One tablespoon chili powder
- One tablespoon paprika
- One tablespoon onion powder

## Directions:
1. Preheat your Airfryer to 390 degrees F.
2. Combine all the ingredients in a mixing bowl. Stir well to distribute ingredients evenly.
3. Place in a heat safe dish and cook for 15 minutes.
4. Serve as a side to your favorite meat or vegetarian meals.

# Easy Garlic Breadsticks

**Prep time: 5 minutes**
**Cooking time: 20 minutes**

**Ingredients:**
- Three cups of bread dough (ready risen and ready for baking)
- Thre tablespoons butter
- Three tablespoons garlic powder

**Directions:**
1. Preheat your Airfryer to 390 degrees F.
2. Roll out the bread dough and cut into strips.
3. Brush with butter and garlic powder.
4. Twist (if so desired) into breadstick twists.
5. Place on a heat safe dish.
6. Bake for twenty minutes. Serve alongside your favorite main meals.

# Cauliflower Breadsticks

**Prep time: 5 minutes**
**Cooking time: 20 minutes**

**Ingredients:**
- One head of cauliflower, lightly cooked and with moisture squeezed from it (either via juicing or using a cheese cloth)
- Four eggs
- One cup cream cheese
- Two cups mozzarella cheese
- One tablespoon black pepper

**Directions:**
1. Preheat your Airfryer to 390 degrees F.
2. Combine all of the ingredients in a food processor or stir thoroughly by hand.
3. Form breadsticks using your hands.
4. Place on a greased oven safe form.
5. Cook in the Air fryer for 20-25 minutes depending on the level of crispiness desired.

# Celeriac Sticks

**Prep time: 5 minutes**
**Cooking time: 20 minutes**

## Ingredients:

- 2 whole celery roots(celeriac), with the outer shell cut off
- 2 eggs, beaten
- One cup chickpea flour
- One tablespoon black pepper

## Directions:

1. Preheat your Airfryer to 390 degrees F.
2. Cut the celeriac into sticks.
3. Combine the chickpea flour and black pepper.
4. Dip the celeriac into the egg mixture and then into the chickpea flour.
5. Place on a greased oven safe dish.
6. Cook in the Air fryer for 18 minutes.

Serve as a side dish in the place of fries.

# Broccoli Flatbread

**Prep time: 5 minutes**
**Cooking time: 20 minutes**

## Ingredients:

- One head of broccoli, florets only lightly cooked and with moisture squeezed from it (either via juicing or using a cheese cloth)
- Four eggs
- One cup cream cheese
- One cup shredded swiss cheese
- One cup cheddar cheese
- One tablespoon black pepper
- Two tablespoons chickpea powder
- One tablespoon garlic powder

## Directions:

1. Preheat your Airfryer to 390 degrees F.
2. Combine all of the ingredients in a food processor or stir thoroughly by hand.
3. Spread out on an oven safe form covered in parchment paper. Spread flat using a spoon.
4. Cook for 20 minutes.

# Almond Flour Breadsticks

**Prep time: 5 minutes**
**Cooking time: 20 minutes**

## Ingredients:

- 4 eggs
- 2 cups almond flour
- One tablespoon baking powder
- One pinch sea salt
- One tablespoon garlic powder
- One teaspoon dried sage
- ½ cup softened butter

## Directions:

1. Preheat your Airfryer to 390 degrees F.
2. Combine all of the ingredients in a food processor or stir  thoroughly by hand.
3. Form breadsticks using your hands.
4. Place on a greased oven safe form.
5. Cook in the Air fryer for 20-25 minutes depending on the level of crispiness desired.
6. Serve with your favorite meals as a low carb, gluten free bread alternative

# Ultimate Twice Baked Stuffed Potato

**Prep time: 5 minutes**
**Cooking time: 25 minutes**

## Ingredients:
- 3 large potatoes
- 3 cups mozzarella cheese
- Two cups sour cream
- One tablespoon cream cheese
- 3 tablespoons garlic powder
- One tablespoon dried or fresh chives
- One tomato, chopped
- One tablespoon olive oil

## Directions:
1. Preheat your Airfryer to 390 degrees F.
2. Brush the potatoes with olive oil.
3. Place them in the Air fryer and cook for 15 minutes.
4. Remove from the Air fryer carefully. Cut a slit in each potato and scoop out most of the potato on the inside of each one.
5. Mix the potato you scooped out of the outside peel with the sour cream, cream cheese, herbs and spices and mozzarella.
6. Scoop the potato back inside the outer casing. It will be fuller now, so rest whatever doesn't fit inside on the top.
7. Place on an oven safe dish and bake for another ten minutes.
8. Enjoy with steak or your favorite meat or veggie meal.

# Bacon Cheese Fries

**Prep time: 5 minutes**
**Cooking time: 23 minutes**

### Ingredients:
- Three potatoes, cut into wedges or lengthwise (fries)
- One tablespoon olive oil
- One pinch sea salt
- One cup bacon, cut into bits
- One cup cheddar cheese

### Directions:
1. Preheat your Airfryer to 390 degrees F.
2. Combine the potatoes with the olive oil in a dish.
3. Add the sea salt. Distribute evenly.
4. Place on a heat safe dish. Cook for 15 minutes.
5. Remove the dish from the Air fryer. Add the bacon and cheddar.
6. Place back in the Air fryer and cook for another 8 minutes.
7. Serve as a delicious side dish.

# Barbeque Cheese Cauliflower

**Prep time: 5 minutes**
**Cooking time: 15 minutes**

### Ingredients:
- One head of cauliflower, cut down into florets
- Two tablespoons olive oil
- One tablespoon black pepper
- One pinch sea salt
- One cup swiss cheese
- Two tablespoons barbeque sauce

### Directions:
1. Preheat your Airfryer to 390 degrees F.
2. Combine the cauliflower florets with the olive oil, black pepper and sea salt.
3. Top with the barbeque sauce and the swiss cheese on a greased, heat safe pan.
4. Place in the Air fryer.
5. Cook for 15 minutes.
6. Serve with your favorite vegetarian or meat-based main meals.

# Garlic Spinach

**Prep time: 5 minutes**
**Cooking time: 8 minutes**

## Ingredients:
- Three cups frozen and thawed and drained spinach
- One cup sour cream
- One tablespoon garlic powder
- One tablespoon olive oil
- Two cloves chopped garlic

## Directions:
1. Preheat your Airfryer to 390 degrees F.
2. Combine all the ingredients in a mixing bowl.
3. Place in a heat safe dish and cook for 8 minutes.
4. Serve alongside your favorite main meals.

# Carrot Garlic Beets

**Prep time: 5 minutes**
**Cooking time: 16 minutes**

## Ingredients:
- Four large carrots, cut into bite-sized pieces
- Two beets, peeled and cut into bite sized pieces
- Three cloves garlic, chopped finely
- One tablespoon garlic powder
- Two tablespoons liquified butter

## Directions:
1. Preheat your Airfryer to 390 degrees F.
2. Place the carrots and beets in a mixing bowl.
3. Mix the liquified butter with the garlic and garlic powder.
4. Pour over the carrots and beets.
5. Use a spoon and/or your hands to be sure the vegetables are well coated in butter.
6. Place in the Air fryer and cook for 16 minutes.
7. Serve alongside your main dish of choice.
8. Combine the potatoes with the olive oil in a dish.

# Stuffed Golden beets

**Prep time: 5 minutes**
**Cooking time: 20 minutes**

**Ingredients:**
- Four large golden beets, peeled
- One cup cream cheese
- ½ cup cooked rice
- One tablespoon garlic powder
- One tablespoon black pepper
- Two tablespoons olive oil

**Directions:**
1. Preheat your Airfryer to 390 degrees F.
2. Cut a hole into each beet so there's space for the stuffing.
3. Combine the rice, cream cheese, garlic and pepper in a mixing bowl.
4. Spoon the combination into each beet.
5. Brush with olive oil.
6. Place on a heat safe dish and cook for 20 minutes.
7. Serve as a side to your favorite meals.

# Parsnip Deluxe Fries with Bacon

**Prep time: 5 minutes**
**Cooking time: 23 minutes**

**Ingredients:**
- Five parsnips, peeled and cut into sticks
- Two tablespoons olive oil
- One cup pepper jack cheese
- One tablespoon black pepper
- One pinch sea salt
- One cup bacon, cut down into bits

**Directions:**
1. Preheat your Airfryer to 390 degrees F.
2. Combine the parsnips with the olive oil, salt and pepper in a dish.
3. Place in a heat safe pan.
4. Top with the cheese and bacon.
5. Fry for 15 minutes.

# Snack

## Broccoli cheddar bites

**Prep time: 10 minutes**
**Cooking time: 10 minutes**

Ingredients:
- 1 head of broccoli, steamed, chopped and de-stemmed
- 1.5 cups shredded cheddar cheese
- 1 tablespoon of olive oil
- 1 pinch of sea salt

Directions:
1. Let the broccoli cool after steaming it. Separate florets from the stem.
2. Combine the broccoli pieces with the cheddar cheese. Preheat your Airfryer to 360 degrees F.
3. Place in a food processor. Pulse for a few seconds.
4. Remove the cheese and broccoli mixture. Form balls with your hands, about a half inch in diameter.
5. Place the broccoli bites in the Airfryer basket. Drizzle with olive oil.
6. Cook for 10 minutes. Remove and sprinkle with salt.
7. Enjoy with a dip of mayonnaise, sour cream or simply as is!

## Easy mozzarella sticks

**Prep time: 5 minutes**
**Cooking time: 10 minutes**

Ingredients:
- 4 unbreaded mozzarella sticks
- 1 cup of breadcrumbs
- 1 egg, beaten

Directions:
1. Preheat the Airfryer to 390 degrees F.
2. Place the beaten egg in a medium sized bowl. Place the breadcrumbs in a separate bowl.
3. Put a mozzarella stick into the egg mixture. Coat the stick evenly and then transfer it to the breadcrumbs. Make sure the mozzarella stick is evenly coated.
4. Repeat the process with all of the mozzarella sticks. Then place them in the Airfryer basket.
5. Airfry for 10 minutes. Serve with marinara sauce.

# Onion Rings

**Prep time: 10 minutes**
**Cooking time: 10 minutes**

## Ingredients:
- 1 large onion
- 1 1/4 cups all-purpose flour
- 1 tsp baking powder
- 1 tsp salt
- 1 egg
- 1 cup milk
- 3/4 cup bread crumbs
- oil for frying

## Directions:
1. Preheat your air fryer to 360 degrees F.
2. Cut onion into 1/4 inch slices and separate onion slices into rings.
3. In a bowl stir flour (previously sifted), salt and baking powder.
4. Dip each onion ring into flour mixture.
5. In another bowl whisk egg with milk and pour it into the flour mixture. Stir until a batter becomes smooth.
6. Dip onion rings in batter.
7. Coat rings with bread crumbs.
8. Put it in air fryer basket.
9. Cook for 7-10 minutes.

# Cheesy fries

**Prep time: 5 minutes**
**Cooking time: 12-15 minutes**

Ingredients:
- 3 large potatoes
- 2 tablespoons of olive oil
- 1/2 teaspoon of salt
- 1.5 cups shredded cheese

**Directions:**
1. Preheat Airfryer to 390 degrees F.
2. Peel (optional) the potatoes. Cut them lengthwise to form wedges (or cut them again to form thin "fry" strips). Place the potato pieces in a bowl with the olive oil and salt. Coat well.
3. Place in the Airfryer basket. Cook for 12-15 minutes, checking on the progress from 12 minutes.
4. Open the Airfryer and put the cheese on the fries. Close the AIrfryer and let the remaining warmth melt the cheese.
5. Remove the fries and serve with the condiments of your choice. (Mayo, bbq sauce, ketchup, etc).

# Kale Chips

**Prep time: 5 minutes**
**Cooking time: 4 minutes**

Ingredients:
- 1 bunch of kale
- 1/2 juiced lemon
- olive oil
- sea salt
- ground pepper to taste

**Directions:**
1. Preheat F.?your air fryer to 320
2. Remove stems from kale and broke it into chip sized pieces.
3. In a bowl stir kale, olive oil and lemon.
4. Put a small layer of kale to the bottom of air fryer basket.
5. Cook for 2-4 minutes.
6. Repeat it for the rest amount of kale.

# Stuffed mushrooms with pesto

**Prep time: 5 minutes**
**Cooking time: 10 minutes**

### Ingredients:
- 3 large portobello mushrooms
- 1 cup of pesto (from a glass or make your own using basil, olive oil, garlic and parmesan cheese in a food processor)
- 1 cup of mozzarella cheese
- 1 tablespoon of olive oil

### Directions:
1. Preheat the Airfryer to 360 degrees F.
2. Fill the mushrooms with pesto and top with cheese.
3. Drizzle with a little olive oil.
4. Put the mushrooms in the Airfryer basket and cook for 10 minutes.
5. Serve with veggie fries and salad as a main meal, or as a side with chicken.

# Zucchini sticks

**Prep time: 5 minutes**
**Cooking time: 10 minutes**

### Ingredients:
- 2 large zucchinis
- 2 tablespoons of olive oil
- 1/2 teaspoon of salt

### Directions:
1. Preheat the Airfryer to 360 degrees F.
2. Cut the zucchini into strips lengthwise. Cut off the ends.
3. Place the zucchini sticks in a bowl with the olive oil and salt and coat well.
4. Put the zucchini in the Airfryer basket and cook for 10 minutes.
5. Remove and enjoy with hummus or guacamole for a healthy and tasty snack or side dish.

# Indian samosas

**Prep time: 15 minutes**
**Cooking time: 12 minutes**

**Ingredients**:
- 2 peeled potatoes
- 0.5 cup of cooked peas (canned or frozen)
- 1 teaspoon Indian spices (curry, turmeric, chilli, salt, pepper, garlic powder, red pepper, fenugreek, ginger)
- 4 frozen pastry dough sheets (croissant dough or another type of pastry may be used)
- 1 tablespoon of olive oil

**Directions:**
1. Preheat the Airfryer to 390 degrees F.
2. Cook and mash the peeled potatoes. Mix the peas in, along with the spices and just a dash of olive oil.
3. Lay the four pastries out and place the potato and pea mix inside. Fold the edges together and pinch the four corners. Brush with olive oil.
4. Place the samosas in the Airfryer basket. Cook for 12 minutes, or until the samosas are golden brown.
5. Serve with chutney as a dip.

# Zucchini Fries with cheese

**Prep time: 10 minutes**
**Cooking time: 20 minutes**

**Ingredients:**
- 3 zucchini (medium sized)
- 2 eggs
- 1/2 cup seasoned bread crumbs
- 2 tbsp grated cheese
- 1/4 tsp garlic powder
- salt
- pepper

**Directions:**
1. Preheat your air fryer to 425 degrees F.
2. Separate egg whites and yolks. Pour egg whites in a bowl and whisk it. Salt and pepper to taste.
3. In another bowl put bread crumbs, cheese & garlic powder. Stir thoroughly.
4. Slice zucchini into sticks.
5. Dip each stick first into the egg whites then into breadcrumbs mixture several times.
6. Put zucchini in air fryer basket.
7. Cook for 15-20 minutes.

# Vegetable fritters

**Prep time: 10 minutes**
**Cooking time: 12 minutes**

Ingredients:
- 1 cup of chickpea flour
- 2 cups of assorted vegetables of your choice (broccoli, peppers, cauliflower, carrots, potatoes, etc)
- 0.5 cup of water
- 1/4 teaspoon chilli powder
- A pinch of garlic powder, salt and pepper

Directions:
1. Preheat the Airfryer to 390 degrees F.
2. Put the chickpea flour in a medium sized mixing bowl along with the water and whisk. Add the spices.
3. Add the vegetables and coat well.
4. Place the vegetables in the Airfryer basket.
5. Cook for 12 minutes.
6. Serve the vegetable fritters with sour cream or sweet and sour sauce

# Beet fries

**Prep time: 5 minutes**
**Cooking time: 12 minutes**

Ingredients:
- 2 cups of washed and peeled beets
- 2 tablespoons of olive oil
- 1 pinch of sea salt

Directions:
1. Preheat the Airfryer to 390 degrees F.
2. Cut the beets into wedges.
3. Combine the beets in a bowl with the olive oil and salt. Toss to coat well.
4. Put the beets in the Airfryer basket and cook for 12 minutes.
5. Serve with sour cream. Also makes an excellent side dish.

# Parsnip fries

**Prep time: 5 minutes**
**Cooking time: 12 minutes**

**Ingredients**:
- 1 large bunch of parsnips (about 5-6 parsnips)
- 2 tablespoons of olive oil
- A pinch of sea salt

**Directions:**
1. Wash and peel the parsnips. Cut them into strips.
2. Place the parsnip strips in a bowl with the olive oil and sea salt. Coat well.
3. Place the parsnip and oil mixture in the Airfryer basket. Cook for 12 minutes.
4. Serve with sour cream or ketchup. Also makes a tasty side dish or addition to a crispy salad.

# Roasted nuts

**Prep time: 5 minutes**
**Cooking time: 12 minutes**

**Ingredients**:
- 2 cups of your choice of nuts (macadamia, peanuts, cashews, hazelnuts, etc.)
- 1 teaspoon of salt
- 0.5 teaspoon of chili powder, pepper, curry, turmeric (your choice of spice blend)
- 2 tablespoons of olive oil

**Directions:**
1. Preheat the Airfryer to 390 degrees F.
2. Put the nuts into a bowl with the oil, salt and spices. Toss to coat evenly.
3. Place the nuts in the Airfryer basket. Roast for 12 minutes.
4. Snack on the nuts throughout the day, take to work, or serve at parties.

# Fried vegetable snacks

**Prep time: 5 minutes**
**Cooking time: 12 minutes**

## Ingredients:
- 2 cups of vegetables (carrots, zucchini, parsnips, beets)
- 2 tablespoons of olive oil
- A pinch of salt and pepper

## Directions:
1. Preheat the Airfryer to 390 degrees F.
2. Wash the vegetables and cut them into bite sized bits.
3. Combine the veggies with oil and salt and pepper.
4. Place the veggies in the Airfryer basket. Cook for 12 minutes.
5. Serve the veggie snacks with your favorite condiments.

# Spicy Onion Rings (low carb)

**Prep time: 6 minutes**
**Cooking time: 18 minutes**

## Ingredients:
- 3 cups onions, sliced to form rings (cut widthwise)
- One egg, beaten
- Two cups almond flour
- One teaspoon black pepper
- One teaspoon chilli powder
- One teaspoon crushed red pepper

## Directions:
1. Preheat your air fryer to 390 degrees F.
2. Combine the dry ingredients in one bowl (the almond flour with the pepper, chili powder and crushed red pepper).
3. Dip the onion rings into the egg mixture then transfer them to the almond flour. Well coat each ring.
4. Place the rings in the Air fryer and cook for 18-20 minutes.
5. Enjoy!

# Zucchini chips
**Prep time: 5 minutes**
**Cooking time: 18 minutes**

**Ingredients:**
- 2 cups thinly sliced zucchini
- Optional: garlic powder, one teaspoon

**Directions:**
1. Preheat your air fryer to 390 degrees F.
2. Combine the thin zucchini slices optionally with whatever herbs and spices you prefer (such as garlic powder, pepper, chili, or salt).
3. Place in the Air fryer and cook for 18 minutes, or until nice and crispy.
4. Serve with salsa or any other kind of dip (guacamole,etc)

# Coconut chips
**Prep time: 5 minutes**
**Cooking time: 6 minutes**

**Ingredients:**
- 2 cups large pieces of shredded coconut
- One tablespoon chili powder
- ⅓ teaspoon coconut sugar (optional)

**Directions:**
1. Preheat your air fryer to 390 degrees F.
2. Combine the shredded coconut pieces with the spices.
3. Cook for just a few minutes in the Air fryer.
4. Enjoy!

# Mini pizza wraps
**Prep time: 5 minutes**
**Cooking time: 12 minutes**

**Ingredients:**
- 5 coconut wraps
- 1 1/2 cups your favorite pizza sauce
- 2 cups shredded mozzarella

**Directions:**
1. Preheat your air fryer to 390 degrees F.
2. Spread the sauce and cheese on each wrap.
3. Wrap up the wraps and cook in the Air fryer for 12 minutes.

# Fish and Seafood

## Barbecued Lime Shrimp (low carb)
**Prep time: 10 minutes**
**Cooking time: 15 minutes**

### Ingredients:
- 4 cups frozen and thawed or fresh shrimp
- 1 1/2 cups barbeque sauce
- One fresh lime, cut into quarters

### Directions:
1. Preheat your air fryer to 360 degrees F.
2. Place the shrimp in a bowl with the barbeque sauce. Stir gently with a spoon. Allow the marinade to sit for at least five minutes (or longer if you have the time).
3. Place in the Air fryer and cook for 15 minutes.
4. Remove from the Air fryer and squeeze with a bit of lime.
5. Enjoy as an appetizer or along with salad for a light and delicious meal.

## Maple Salmon
**Prep time: 5 minutes**
**Cooking time: 14 minutes**

### Ingredients:
- One pound of salmon filets, cut into portions
- 4 tablespoons maple syrup
- One tablespoon olive oil
- One teaspoon black pepper

### Directions:
1. Preheat your air fryer to 390 degrees F.
2. Place the maple syrup, olive oil and black pepper in a bowl. Stir with a spoon to combine evenly.
3. Place each salmon filet one at a time into the marinade. Turn each filet to coat both sides.
4. Put the salmon in the Air fryer basket. Cook for 14 minutes or until a nice golden brown.

# Brown sugar glazed salmon

**Prep time: 5 minutes**
**Cooking time: 15 minutes**

**Ingredients**:
- 3 salmon filets
- 1 tablespoon brown sugar
- 2 tablespoons of coconut oil, melted to a liquid
- A pinch of salt and pepper

**Directions:**
1. Preheat the Airfryer to 360 degrees F.
2. Combine the coconut oil with the brown sugar and salt and pepper in a medium sized bowl.
3. Place the salmon filets in the bowl. Cover with the glaze. Pour the mixture over the salmon with a spoon taking care to not cut up the salmon in the process.
4. Put the glazed salmon in the Airfryer. Cook for about 15 minutes, checking progress from 12 minutes on.
5. Serve with your choice of vegetable fries and salad.

# Stuffed Zander Filets

**Prep time: 10 minutes**
**Cooking time: 14 minutes**

**Ingredients:**
- 4 zander filets
- One cup goat cheese
- One tablespoon dried dill
- One tablespoon olive oil

**Directions:**
1. Preheat your air fryer to 390 degrees F.
2. Cut each zander filet through the middle lengthwise so you can open them like a book.
3. Put a spoonful of goat cheese in the middle. Sprinkle with dill. Brush with olive oil.
4. Place in the Air fryer and cook for 14 minutes.
5. Enjoy!

# Low Carb Fish Filets
**Prep time: 8 minutes**
**Cooking time: 18 minutes**

**Ingredients:**
- 4 fish filets of your choice of white fish
- One cup almond flour
- One egg, beaten
- 1/4 teaspoon black pepper

**Directions:**
1. Preheat your air fryer to 390 degrees F.
2. Put the almond flour, pepper into one bowl and stir well to combine.
3. Dip each filet into first the egg mixture, and then into the almond mixture and then into the Air fryer basket.
4. Cook for 15-18 minutes.
5. Enjoy with salad for a low carb meal or Air fryer fries for a meal kids love. (Like fish sticks but much healthier!)

---

# Breaded Buckwheat Salmon (gluten free, lower carb)
**Prep time: 8 minutes**
**Cooking time: 16 minutes**

**Ingredients:**
- 4 salmon filets
- 1 1/2 cups buckwheat flour
- 1 egg, beaten
- 1/4 teaspoon black pepper
- 1/2 teaspoon garlic powder

**Directions:**
1. Preheat your air fryer to 390 degrees F.
2. Combine the buckwheat flour with the pepper and garlic powder in a medium sized mixing bowl.
3. Place each salmon filet in the bowl with beaten egg. Coat both sides.
4. Transfer to the bowl with the buckwheat spice mixture and coat both sides of each fish filet.
5. Transfer on to the Air fryer basket. When all four filets have been coated with egg and the buckwheat mixture, place in the Air fryer.
6. Cook for 16-18 minutes.

# Crab Wraps

**Prep time: 7 minutes**
**Cooking time: 10 minutes**

## Ingredients:
- 2 cups crab meat
- 1 teaspoon garlic powder
- 2 tablespoons mayonaise
- One tablespoon lemon juice
- 2 low carb wraps
- 1/2 cup ice berg lettuce, chopped

## Directions:
1. Preheat your air fryer to 390 degrees F.
2. Place the crap meat in the Air fryer basket and cook for 10 minutes.
3. In the meantime, mix the mayonnaise dressing with the lemon juice and garlic.
4. Prepare the wraps by putting 1/4 cup lettuce on each wrap.
5. Remove the crab meat from the Air fryer. Mix with the mayonnaise dressing and spoon onto the wraps.
6. Enjoy this easy seafood meal.

# Low Carb Crab Cakes

**Prep time: 10 minutes**
**Cooking time: 18 minutes**

## Ingredients:
- 4 cups crab meat
- 2 eggs, beaten
- 1/2 teaspoon black pepper
- 1 1/2 cup almond meal

## Directions:
1. Preheat your air fryer to 390 degrees F.
2. With an electric hand mixer (can also be done by hand but will be a different consistency) mix the crab meat and eggs and black pepper.
3. With your hands, form the crab and egg mixture into balls.
4. "Roll" each ball in the almond meal to coat. Repeat with all of the crab mixture.
5. Place the crab cakes in the Air fryer basket and cook for 18 minutes.
6. Enjoy with tartar sauce, sour cream or mayonnaise and a side of beet fries or a salad.

# Crispy Prawns
**Prep time: 10 minutes**
**Cooking time: 10 minutes**

**Ingredients:**
- 12 prawns (cleaned, washed and dried)
- salt
- freshly ground pepper
- 2 eggs
- 7 oz spicy chips

**Directions:**
1. Preheat your air fryer to 350 degrees F.
2. Season prawns with pinch of salt and pepper.
3. Separate egg whites and yolks. Pour egg whites in a bowl.
4. Crush chips in another bowl.
5. Dip each prawn first in the egg and then in the chips crumbs.
6. Put prawns in airfryer basket.
7. Bake for 8-10 minutes until they become brown

# Air Fryer Crab Rangoons (gluten free and low carb variation included)
**Prep time: 5 minutes**
**Cooking time: 15 minutes**

**Ingredients:**
- 8 sheets of pastry dough (substitute with low carb coconut wraps if desired)
- 3 cups cream cheese
- One cup crab meat
- 1/4 teaspoon black pepper
- 1/4 teaspoon sea salt
- 1/4 teaspoon chili powder
- One egg, beaten

**Directions:**
8. Preheat your air fryer to 390 degrees F.
9. In a bowl, stir together the crab meat, cream cheese, black pepper, sea salt and chili powder.
10. Lay out the pastries (or wraps) and spoon in the cream cheese and crab mixture.
11. Brush egg on the edges and fold together to form crab rangoons.
12. Place in the Air fryer and fry for 15 minutes.
13. Serve with sweet and sour sauce or your choice of dip.

# Crumbed Fish

**Prep time: 10 minutes**
**Cooking time: 12 minutes**

Ingredients:
- 4 tbsp vegetable oil
- 3.5 oz bread crumbs
- 1 egg
- 4 fish fillets (medium thickness)

Directions:
1. Preheat your air fryer to 350 degrees F.
2. In a bowl, combine bread crumbs and oil. Stir it.
3. Whisk the egg.
4. Dip the fish first in the egg and then in crumbs mixture.
5. Put in air fryer basket.
6. Cook for 12 minutes

# Salmon Samosas (low carb and gluten free)

**Prep time: 10 minutes**
**Cooking time: 12 minutes**

Ingredients:
- 4 coconut wraps (low carb wraps)
- 1 1/2 cup salmon meat, cooked
- 1 cup celeriac, cooked and cut into bite-sized pieces
- 1 cup shredded carrots
- 1/2 teaspoon ginger powder
- 1/2 teaspoon black pepper
- 1/2 teaspoon garlic powder
- One egg, beaten

Directions:
1. Preheat your air fryer to 390 degrees F.
2. In a bowl, combine the salmon meat, celeriac, carrots, ginger, pepper and garlic powder. (Stir, don't crush)
3. Spoon the mixture onto each coconut wrap.
4. Roll up the wraps to form samosas and brush with the beaten egg.
5. Place in the Air fryer and cook for 12 minutes. Serve with sour cream.

# Cajun Shrimp

**Prep time: 5 minutes**
**Cooking time: 5 minutes**

## Ingredients:

- 18-20 tiger shrimps
- 1/4 tsp cayenne pepper
- 1/2 tsp seasoning
- 1/4 tsp smoked paprika
- salt
- 1 tbsp olive oil

## Directions:

1. Preheat your air fryer to 390 degrees F.
2. In a bowl, mix pinch of salt, pepper and seasoning.
3. Dip each shrimp first into olive oil and then in seasoning mixture.
4. Put shrimps in air fryer basket.
5. Cook for 5 minutes

# Low Carb Cod Filets

**Prep time: 8 minutes**
**Cooking time: 16 minutes**

## Ingredients:

- 4 cod filets, fresh or frozen and thawed
- One egg, beaten
- 2 cups almond meal
- 1 teaspoon black pepper
- 1/2 teaspoon garlic powder
- 1/2 teaspoon thyme

## Directions:

1. Preheat your air fryer to 390 degrees F.
2. Combine the almond meal, pepper, garlic and thyme in a bowl together.
3. Place each filet into the egg mixture. Then transfer to the almond meal. Make sure each filet is well-coated.
4. Place in the Air fryer and cook for 16 minutes. Serve with salad for a low carb meal or with potatoes and carrots for a more hearty family dinner.

# Cheesy Fish Fingers

**Prep time: 5 minutes**
**Cooking time: 25 minutes**

**Ingredients:**
- Five filets of white fish, cut into "fingers" (cod for example)
- Two eggs, beaten
- One cup cream cheese, softened
- Three cups almond flour

**Directions:**
1. Preheat your Airfryer to 390 degrees F.
2. First coat each fish stick in the beaten egg mixture by dipping them in the mixing bowl where the beaten egg is.
3. Spread the softened cream cheese careful on the top of each fish filet.
4. Then dip into the almond flour. Be sure to coat all sides evenly.
5. Place on a greased, heat safe dish.
6. Cook for 25 minutes.

# Fried Garlic Butter Clams and Beets

**Prep time: 5 minutes**
**Cooking time: 18 minutes**

**Ingredients:**
- Two cups clams in clam juice
- Two beets, cut into bite sized pieces
- Three tablespoons butter, warmed to liquid
- One tablespoon black pepper
- One tablespoon garlic powder
- One chopped garlic clove

**Directions:**
1. Preheat your Airfryer to 390 degrees F.
2. Gently stir the ingredients together, taking care to evenly distribute the butter and herbs and spices.
3. Place in a heat safe dish.
4. Cook in the Air fryer for 18 minutes.

# Mustard Salmon Filet

**Prep time: 15 minutes**
**Cooking time: 30 minutes**

## Ingredients:
- 2 large salmon filets
- 2 tbsp olive oil
- 2 tbsp mustard
- ¼ tsp pepper

## Directions:
1. Preheat your air fryer to 400 °F.
2. Combine the olive oil and mustard in a dish along with the pepper.
3. Place each salmon filet in the marinade. Turn to coat.
4. Place in the Air fryer and cook for 30 minutes.

# Coconut Shrimp

**Prep time: 5 minutes**
**Cooking time: 25 minutes**

## Ingredients:
- Two cups shrimp, peeled with the tails removed
- ½ cup coconut milk
- One tablespoon corn starch
- One tablespoon black pepper
- One teaspoon lemongrass powder
- One pinch sea salt

## Directions:
1. Preheat your Airfryer to 390 degrees F.
2. Mix together the coconut milk, corn starch, pepper, lemongrass powder and sea salt.
3. Then add the shrimp.
4. Place in a heat safe dish and cook in the Air fryer for 25 minutes.

# Swordfish Barbeque Filet

**Prep time: 15 minutes**
**Cooking time: 30 minutes**

**Ingredients:**
- 2 large swordfish filets
- 2 tbsp olive oil
- 2 tbsp barbeque sauce
- ¼ tsp pepper

**Directions:**
1. Preheat your air fryer to 390 degrees F
2. Combine the olive oil and barbeque sauce in a dish along with the pepper.
3. Place each swordfish filet in the marinade. Turn to coat.
4. Place in the Air fryer and cook for 30 minutes.

# Shrimp and Sweet Mayonnaise

**Prep time: 15 minutes**
**Cooking time: 30 minutes**

**Ingredients:**
- 4 cups peeled shrimp
- 2 tbsp olive oil
- One cup quinoa flour
- ¼ tsp pepper
- One cup mayonnaise
- One tablespoon coconut sugar
- One tablespoon chili powder

**Directions:**
1. Preheat your air fryer to 390 degrees F.
2. Coat the shrimp with olive oil.
3. Then place in the dish with quinoa flour and coat.
4. Put in the air fryer and cook for 30 minutes.
5. In the meantime, mix the mayonnaise by combining the chili with the coconut sugar and mayonnaise.
6. Serve the shrimp with the may as a dip.

# Pesto Cod

**Prep time: 15 minutes**
**Cooking time: 30 minutes**

## Ingredients:
- 2 large cod filets
- 2 tbsp olive oil
- 2 tbsp pesto
- ¼ tsp pepper

## Directions:
1. Preheat your air fryer to 390 degrees F.
2. Combine the olive oil and pesto in a dish along with the pepper.
3. Place each cod filet in the mixture of olive oil and pesto and turn to coat.
4. Place in the Air fryer and cook for 30 minutes.

# Cheddar Crabcakes

**Prep time: 15 minutes**
**Cooking time: 30 minutes**

## Ingredients:
- 2 cups crabmeat
- 2 cups shredded cheddar cheese
- 1 cup almond flour
- 1 tbsp olive oil
- ¼ tsp pepper

## Directions:
1. Preheat your air fryer to 390 degrees F.
2. Combine the crabmeat and cheddar cheese in a mixing bowl.
3. Form balls with the meat and cheese mixture using your hands.
4. Coat the balls in olive oil first and then roll in the almond flour to coat well.
5. Place in the Air fryer and cook for 30 minutes. Serve with the dipping sauce of your choice.

# Lobster Celeriac Filet

**Prep time: 15 minutes**
**Cooking time: 30 minutes**

**Ingredients:**
- 2 cups lobster meat
- 2 tbsp olive oil
- 2 cups shredded celeriac (use a cheese grater to grate)
- ¼ tsp pepper

**Directions:**
1. Preheat your air fryer to 390 degrees F.
2. Combine the oil, celeriac, pepper and lobster meat in a bowl. Stir using your hands and/or a large wooden spoon.
3. Form flat pancake like filets using spoon and parchment paper.
4. Place the filets in the air fryer and cook for 30 minutes.

# Cheesy Salmon Cakes

**Prep time: 15 minutes**
**Cooking time: 20 minutes**

**Ingredients:**
- 2 cups cooked salmon meat
- 2 cups shredded swiss cheese
- ½ cup cream cheese
- 2 tbsp olive oil
- ¼ tsp pepper
- 1 cups shredded parsley

**Directions:**
1. Preheat your air fryer to 390 degrees F.
2. In a mixing bowl, place the salmon, cheese, cream cheese,parsley, pepper and olive oil. Use your hands or a wooden spoon to combine.
3. Use your hands to form cakes (patties).
4. Place in the Air fryer and cook for 20 minutes until cheese is deliciously melted. Serve with salad and/or bread.

# Cajun Shrimp

**Prep time: 5 minutes**
**Cooking time: 5 minutes**

## Ingredients:

- 18-20 tiger shrimps
- 1/4 tsp cayenne pepper
- 1/2 tsp seasoning
- 1/4 tsp smoked paprika
- salt
- 1 tbsp olive oil

## Directions:

6. Preheat your air fryer to 390 degrees F.
7. In a bowl, mix pinch of salt, pepper and seasoning.
8. Dip each shrimp first into olive oil and then in seasoning mixture.
9. Put shrimps in air fryer basket.
10. Cook for 5 minutes

# Seafood Veggie Fritters

**Prep time: 15 minutes**
**Cooking time: 30 minutes**

## Ingredients:

- 2 cups clam meat
- 1 cup shredded carrot
- ½ cup shredded zucchini
- One cup chickpea flour, combined with ¾ cup water to form batter
- 2 tbsp olive oil
- ¼ tsp pepper

## Directions:

1. Preheat your air fryer to 390 degrees F.
2. Combine the clam meat, olive oil, shredded carrot and zucchini along with the pepper in a mixing bowl. Form small balls using your hands.
3. Coat the balls with the chickpea mixture.
4. Place in the air fryer and cook for 30 minutes or until nice and crispy.

# Salmon Cauliflower Balls

**Prep time: 15 minutes**
**Cooking time: 30 minutes**

**Ingredients:**
- 2 cups cooked salmon
- 1 head cauliflower, steamed and cut into smaller florets
- 2 cups chickpea flour
- 2 tbsp olive oil
- 1 tsp garlic powder
- ¼ tsp pepper

**Directions:**
1. Preheat your air fryer to 390 degrees F.
2. In a medium sized bowl, combine the cauliflower, salmon, garlic powder and pepper. Stir well to distribute evenly. (You may use a hand mixer if you would like a smoother consistency)
3. Use your hands to form balls.
4. Place the olive oil in a dish and roll the balls in the oil.
5. Roll the balls in the chickpea flour to coat well.
6. Fry in the air fryer for 25 minutes.
7. Serve with a spicy mayonnaise or tzaziki and salad.

# Shrimp Rolls

**Prep time: 5 minutes**
**Cooking time: 10 minutes**

**Ingredients:**
- 5 sheets of rice "paper" (egg roll sheets)
- two eggs, beaten
- One tablespoon onion powder
- One tablespoon garlic powder
- 1 cup cream cheese
- One cup shredded purple cabbage
- ½ cup shredded carrots
- One cup shrimp, peeled with tails removed

**Directions:**
1. Preheat your Airfryer to 390 degrees F.
2. Mix the cheese, cabbage, carrots, shrimp and the onion and garlic powder.
3. Dip each rice "paper" in lukewarm water and remove quickly. Spread flat on a clean surface.
4. Distribute the shrimp mix evenly among the rice sheets.
5. Wrap up and fold over the rice rolls.
6. Dip in the egg mix.
7. Place on a greased, heat safe form and cook in the Air fryer for 10 minutes.
8. Serve with sweet and sour sauce or chutney and sour cream as a side or as a snack or small meal.

# Crab Spinach Rangoons

**Prep time: 5 minutes**
**Cooking time: 18 minutes**

## Ingredients:
- 4 sheets of flaky pastry dough (filo works well)
- 2 cups cream cheese
- ½ cup spinach, frozen and thawed and drained of extra moisture
- ½ cup crabmeat
- 2 cloves garlic, chopped finely
- 2 tablespoons olive oil
- One egg, beaten

## Directions:
1. Preheat your Airfryer to 390 degrees F.
2. In a medium sized mixing bowl, combine the crab, spinach, garlic, cheese, and one tablespoon of olive oil.
3. Spoon some of the mixture onto each pastry. Fold and tuck in the ends. Brush with the egg to make the ends stick.
4. Brush the tops of each pastry with olive oil.
5. Cut small slits into each pastry.
6. Air fry for 18 minutes.

# Mustard Salmon in Flaky Dough

**Prep time: 5 minutes**
**Cooking time: 20 minutes**

## Ingredients:
- 4 sheets of flaky pastry dough (filo works well)
- 4 small filets of salmon
- Two tablespoons sweet mustard
- One egg, beaten
- ½ cup butter, warmed to a liquid

## Directions:
1. Preheat your Airfryer to 390 degrees F.
2. Place each salmon filet on its own pastry dough sheet.
3. Spread about ½ tablespoon of mustard onto the top of each salmon filet
4. Fold over the pastry. Brush the ends with egg to seal.
5. Brush with butter over the top.
6. Place in the Air fryer and cook for 20 minutes.

# Cheesy Breaded Salmon

**Prep time: 5 minutes**
**Cooking time: 20 minutes**

### Ingredients:
- 2 cups breadcrumbs
- 4 filets of salmon
- One cup swiss cheese, shredded
- Two eggs, beaten

### Directions:
1. Preheat your Airfryer to 390 degrees F.
2. Dip each salmon filet into the egg mixture.
3. Top with swiss cheese.
4. Dip into the breadcrumbs and coat all sides of the fish.
5. Place on an oven safe dish and cook for 20 minutes.

# Cod Rolls

**Prep time: 5 minutes**
**Cooking time: 10 minutes**

### Ingredients:
- 5 sheets of rice "paper" (egg roll sheets)
- two eggs, beaten
- One tablespoon onion powder
- One tablespoon garlic powder
- One cup cooked cod, cut into pieces
- ½ cup shredded zucchini
- ½ cup shredded white cabbage
- ½ cup shredded swiss cheese
- 1 tablespoon sour cream

### Directions:
1. Preheat your Airfryer to 390 degrees F.
2. Mix the cheese, cabbage, zucchini, cod and the onion and garlic powder.
3. Dip each rice "paper" in lukewarm water and remove quickly. Spread flat on a clean surface.
4. Distribute the fish mix evenly among the rice sheets.
5. Wrap up and fold over the rice rolls.
6. Dip in the egg mix.
7. Place on a greased, heat safe form and cook in the Air fryer for 10 minutes.
8. Serve with sweet and sour sauce or chutney and sour cream as a side or as a snack or small meal.

# Bacon Fried Cod

**Prep time: 5 minutes**
**Cooking time: 25 minutes**

### Ingredients:
- 2 cod filets
- 6 strips of bacon

### Directions:
1. Preheat your Airfryer to 390 degrees F.
2. Wrap 3 slices of bacon around each cold filet.
3. Place on a heat safe dish and cook for 25 minutes.

# Lobster Wrap

**Prep time: 5 minutes**
**Cooking time: 14 minutes**

### Ingredients:
- 2 cups lobster meat
- One celery stalk, very finely chopped
- One onion, finely chopped
- One cup mayonaise
- 4 wraps (gluten free, low carb or whole wheat)
- One egg, beaten

### Directions:
1. Preheat your Airfryer to 390 degrees F.
2. Combine the lobster meat, celery, onion and mayonaise in a mixing bowl using a large spoon.
3. Spread out onto each wrap.
4. Fold the wrap and brush with egg.
5. Place in the Air fryer and cook for 14 minutes.

# Rice Crab Rolls

**Prep time: 5 minutes**
**Cooking time: 10 minutes**

## Ingredients:
- 5 sheets of rice "paper" (egg roll sheets)
- two eggs, beaten
- One tablespoon onion powder
- One tablespoon garlic powder
- 1 ½ cups crab meat
- ½ cup herbed cream cheese
- Two tablespoons scallions
- ½ cup shredded carrots.

## Directions:
1. Preheat your Airfryer to 390 degrees F.
2. Mix the cheese, carrots, crab and the onion and garlic powder.
3. Dip each rice "paper" in lukewarm water and remove quickly. Spread flat on a clean surface.
4. Distribute the fish mix evenly among the rice sheets.
5. Wrap up and fold over the rice rolls.
6. Dip in the egg mix.
7. Place on a greased, heat safe form and cook in the Air fryer for 10 minutes.

# Swordfish sticks

**Prep time: 5 minutes**
**Cooking time: 25 minutes**

## Ingredients:
- Two filets (steaks) of swordfish, cut into "fingers" by slicing lengthwise
- Two eggs, beaten
- Two cups chickpea flour
- One tablespoon garlic powder
- One tablespoon black pepper

## Directions:
1. Preheat your Airfryer to 390 degrees F.
2. First coat each fish stick in the beaten egg mixture by dipping them in the mixing bowl where the beaten egg is.
3. Then dip into the almond flour. Be sure to coat all sides evenly.
4. Place on a greased, heat safe dish.
5. Cook for 25 minutes.

# Seafood stuffed peppers

**Prep time: 5 minutes**
**Cooking time: 20 minutes**

## Ingredients:

- 3 red bell peppers with the tops cut off and insides removed
- ½ cup cooked shrimp with tails removed
- 1 cup cooked salmon, cut into small pieces
- ½ cup cooked rice
- ½ cup cream cheese
- One tablespoon garlic powder
- One tablespoon black pepper
- One tablespoon chopped green onions
- One tablespoon olive oil.
- One cup shredded cheddar cheese

## Directions:

1. Preheat your Airfryer to 390 degrees F.
2. Mix the shrimp, salmon, rice, cream cheese, garlic, pepper and green onions in a medium-sized mixing bowl.
3. Scoop the mixture into each of the peppers.
4. Brush with olive oil.
5. Top with the cheddar cheese (onto each pepper)
6. Place in the Air fryer and cook for 20 minutes.

# Tunafish Tomatoes (stuffed tomatoes)

**Prep time: 5 minutes**
**Cooking time: 12 minutes**

## Ingredients:

- 5 beefsteak (large) tomatoes, tops sliced off and insides scooped out
- 2 cups tuna fish
- ½ cup cream cheese
- One teaspoon lemon juice
- One tablespoon sour cream
- One celery stalk, finely chopped
- One cup swiss cheese, shredded

## Directions:

1. Preheat your Airfryer to 390 degrees F.
2. Mix the tuna fish, cream cheese, lemon juice, sour cream and celery in a medium sized bowl.
3. Spoon the tuna fish mixture into each of the tomatoes.
4. Top with the shredded swiss cheese.

5.   Cook in the Air fryer for 12 minutes.

# Airfryer Fish Tacos

**Prep time: 5 minutes**
**Cooking time: 18 minutes**

**Ingredients:**
- 2 cups white fish
- Two tablespoons chili powder
- One tablespoon black pepper
- One tablespoon garlic powder
- One tablespoon paprika
- One teaspoon fenugreek
- One tablespoon olive oil
- 4 taco shells
- One cup shredded lettuce
- One cup spicy cheese (shredded)
- One cup chopped tomatoes
- One cup taco sauce.

**Directions:**
1. Preheat your Airfryer to 390 degrees F.
2. Combine the fish with the chili, pepper, garlic, paprika, fenugreek and olive oil.
3. Place on a heat safe dish and cook for 15 minutes.
4. Place in the taco shells and cook for 3 more minutes.
5. Top with the rest of the toppings and enjoy.

# Tillapia in Pineapple Coconut Sauce

**Prep time: 5 minutes**
**Cooking time: 20 minutes**

**Ingredients:**
- 3 filets of tilapia
- One cup pineapple slices
- One cup coconut milk
- One tablespoon black pepper
- One tablespoon corn starch

**Directions:**
1. Preheat your Airfryer to 390 degrees F.
2. In a food processor, combine the pineapple with the coconut milk, black pepper and corn starch.
3. Place in an oven safe form along with the fish.
4. Cook for 20 minutes.

# Fried Mushroom Trout

**Prep time: 5 minutes**
**Cooking time: 20 minutes**

**Ingredients:**
- 3 filets of trout
- One cup sliced mushrooms
- One cup sour cream
- One tablespoon black pepper
- One tablespoon corn starch

**Directions:**
1. Preheat your Airfryer to 390 degrees F.
2. In a bowl, combine the mushrooms with the sour cream, black pepper and corn starch.
3. Place in an oven safe form along with the fish.
4. Cook for 20 minutes.

# Shrimp and Mushrooms

**Prep time: 5 minutes**
**Cooking time: 15 minutes**

**Ingredients:**
- 3 cups of shrimp, peeled with tales removed
- Two cups sliced mushrooms
- One cup coconut milk
- One tablespoon black pepper
- One tablespoon corn starch

**Directions:**
1. Preheat your Airfryer to 390 degrees F.
5. In a bowl, combine the mushrooms with the coconut milk, black pepper and corn starch.
6. Place in an oven safe form along with the shrimp.
7. Cook for 15 minutes.

# Cranberry Cod

**Prep time: 5 minutes**
**Cooking time: 20 minutes**

## Ingredients:
- 3 filets of cod
- 3 tablespoons lingonberry or cranberry jam
- One tablespoon olive oil

## Directions:
1. Preheat your Airfryer to 390 degrees F.
2. Brush each cod filet with olive oil.
3. Spoon one tablespoon of cranberry jam on top of each filet.
4. Cook for 20 minutes.

# Clam chowder bread bowl

**Prep time: 5 minutes**
**Cooking time: 18 minutes**

## Ingredients:
- One round loaf of bread (home baked is best but any round bread loaf will do)
- Two cups whole milk
- One cup clams (in juice)
- ½ cup shredded carrots
- One tablespoon vegetable boullion
- One tablespoon black pepper
- Two cups swiss cheese

## Directions:
1. Preheat your Airfryer to 390 degrees F.
2. Heat the milk, clams, carrots, boullion and black pepper over the stove on medium heat for three minutes.
3. Whisk the boullion to be sure it dissolves evenly.
4. Cut the top off the round bread loaf and scoop out just enough bread (leaving enough on the bottom) to form a bowl.
5. Spoon the soup in.
6. Top with the cheese and cook for 18 minutes.

# Poultry

## Low Carb Chicken Fingers
**Prep time: 8 minutes**
**Cooking time: 18 minutes**

### Ingredients:
- 2 breasts of chicken, cut into strips
- One egg, beaten
- 1 teaspoon black pepper
- One cup almond flour
- 1 teaspoon dill

### Directions:
1. Preheat your air fryer to 390 degrees F.
2. Combine the black pepper with the dill and the almond flour in a medium-sized mixing bowl.
3. Dip the chicken strips in the beaten egg first. Then transfer to the almond mixture. Be sure to coat all sides of the chicken with the egg and the almond flour.
4. Place in the Air fryer and cook for 18-20 minutes. Serve with your favorite sauce (barbeque, ketchup, etc.) and a salad for a low carb meal.

## Chicken and cream sauce
**Prep time: 5 minutes**
**Cooking time: 15-18 minutes**

### Ingredients:
- 2 chicken skinless chicken breasts
- 1/2 cup cream
- A pinch of salt and pepper
- 1/2 tablespoon of olive oil

### Directions:
1. Preheat the Airfryer to 360 degrees F.
2. Put the cream in a medium-sized bowl with the olive oil and the salt and pepper and mix.
3. Put the chicken in an oven safe dish and pour in the contents of the bowl.
4. Place in the Airfryer and cook for 15 minutes. Check on the chicken and cook for 3 more minutes if necessary.
Garnish with fresh basil. Serve with beet fries and salad.

# Stuffed Turkey

**Prep time: 8-10 minutes**
**Cooking time: 22 minutes**

## Ingredients:
- 2 turkey breasts, cut lengthwise through the middle but left attached (so can be opened like a book)
- 2 tablespoons sour cream
- 2 tablespoons cranberry sauce (or lingonberry jam)

## Directions:
1. Preheat your air fryer to 390 degrees F.
2. Put a tablespoon of sour cream and a tablespoon of cranberry sauce into the middle of each turkey breast. (In between where you made the lengthwise cuts) Put the sides back together.
3. Place in the Air fryer and cook for 22 minutes or until fully roasted.
4. Serve with steamed broccoli and carrots for a warm and delicious fall and winter meal.

# Healthier Fried Chicken

**Prep time: 8 minutes**
**Cooking time: 20 minutes**

## Ingredients:
- One pound chicken legs, wings and breasts
- 2 cups almond flour
- 1 teaspoon paprika powder
- 1 teaspoon chili powder
- 2 teaspoons black pepper
- Two eggs, beaten

## Directions:
1. Preheat your air fryer to 390 degrees F.
2. Mix the almond flour, paprika, chili and black pepper in a bowl.
3. Place the chicken in the egg mixture. Coat well and transfer to the almond mixture and coat well.
4. Repeat until all of the chicken has been breaded.
5. Place in the Air fryer and cook for 20 minutes. Serve with ranch sauce.

# Fried chicken

**Prep time: 5 minutes**
**Cooking time: 15-18 minutes**

Ingredients:
- Half a pound of chicken wings, breasts and legs
- 1 cup of your favorite chicken marinade (barbeque sauce, etc)

Directions:
1. Preheat the Airfryer to 360 degrees F.
2. Put the chicken into a large mixing bowl along with the marinade. Combine evenly.
3. Place the chicken and marinade mixture into the Airfryer basket.
4. Fry for 15-18 minutes, checking periodically.
5. Serve with sweet potato fries and sour cream and salad for a complete dinner or larger lunch.

# Chicken Parmesan

**Prep time: 8 minutes**
**Cooking time: 24 minutes**

Ingredients:
- 2 chicken breasts, boneless
- 1/2 cup tomato sauce
- 1 cup shredded mozzarella cheese
- 2 leaves of basil

Directions:
1. Preheat your air fryer to 390 degrees F.
2. Place the chicken breasts in the Air fryer. Cook for 10 minutes.
3. Remove and cut lengthwise. Top with a bit of tomato sauce and basil. Finally, top off with the mozzarella cheese.
4. Put back into the Air fryer. Cook for 14 more minutes.
5. Enjoy with a salad or zucchini noodles.

# Tempting Turkey

**Prep time: 8 minutes**
**Cooking time: 20 minutes**

## Ingredients:
- 2 large turkey breasts
- One tablespoon coconut sugar
- One teaspoon black pepper
- One tablespoon olive oil
- One tomato, sliced
- One cup swiss cheese

## Directions:
1. Preheat your air fryer to 390 degrees F.
2. In a mixing bowl, combine coconut sugar with the pepper and olive oil.
3. Cut each turkey lengthwise but leave attached at the end. Put sliced tomato and swiss cheese in between the cut sides of the turkey breasts.
4. Coat with the coconut sugar and olive oil mixture.
5. Place in the Air fryer and cook for 20-25 minutes or until cooked through.

# Chicken Drumsticks

**Prep time: 2 minutes**
**Cooking time: 20 minutes**

## Ingredients:
- 4 pcs drumsticks
- 1 tsp oil
- salt
- pepper

## Directions:
1. Preheat your air fryer to 390 degrees F.
2. Put drumsticks into air fryer and cook for 10 minutes.
3. Sprinkle them with oil, salt & pepper.
4. Reduce temperature to 300 degrees F.
5. Cook 10 minutes.

# Chicken Rolls (low carb, gluten free)
**Prep time: 7 minutes**
**Cooking time: 12 minutes**

## Ingredients:
- 4 coconut wraps (or other gluten free, low carb wraps)
- 1 1/2 cup chicken strips
- One cup shredded carrots
- One teaspoon garlic powder
- One green pepper, chopped
- One onion, chopped
- One egg, beaten

## Directions:
1. Preheat your air fryer to 390 degrees F.
2. In a medium sized bowl, combine the chicken, shredded carrots, garlic powder, peppers and onions. Stir to combine evenly.
3. Spoon the mixture into the four wraps. Roll up the wraps.
4. Brush the egg between the edges of the wraps to seal.
5. Place in the Air fryer and cook for 12 minutes.

# Turkey Wraps
**Prep time: 5 minutes**
**Cooking time: 8 minutes**

## Ingredients:
- One cup turkey strips
- 4 gluten free wraps
- One tablespoon mayonaise
- One tablespoon pesto
- 1/2 cup tomato sauce
- One cup shredded zucchini (use cheese grater)

## Directions:
1. Preheat your air fryer to 390 degrees F.
2. Mix together the turkey, pesto and tomato sauce and zucchini. Place in the Air fryer. Cook for 8 minutes
3. Spread the wraps with the mayo.
4. Remove the turkey mixture and spoon into each wrap. Wrap up and enjoy!

# Chicken Wrapped In Bacon
**Prep time: 3 minutes**
**Cooking time: 15 minutes**

## Ingredients:
- 6 bacon rashers
- 1 chicken breast
- 1 tbsp garlic cheese

## Directions:
1. Preheat your air fryer to 350 degrees F.
2. Cut chicken breast.
3. In a bowl make a marinade - mix oil, Maggi sauce, fish and soy sauce.
4. Melt goose fat in microwave.
5. Pour the marinade into the bowl with tofu. Stir it.
6. Set aside for 30 minutes. Stir it a few times.
7. Put tofu in air fryer basket.
8. Cook for 8-10 minutes.
9. Turn tofu or shake it.
10. Cook for additional 8-10 minutes

# Roast Orange Duck
**Prep time: 10 minutes**
**Cooking time: 18 minutes**

## Ingredients:
- 3 cups duck breast, cut into bite-sized pieces
- One tablespoon coconut oil, warmed to liquid
- One teaspoon chili powder
- One teaspoon garlic powder
- One teaspoon black pepper
- One teaspoon orange juice

## Directions:
1. Preheat your air fryer to 390 degrees F.
2. In a mixing bowl, combine coconut oil, chili powder, garlic, pepper and orange juice.
3. Add the duck and allow to marinate for five minutes (or longer if you have the time)
4. Place in the Air fryer and cook for 18 minutes. Serve with a side of cauliflower "rice".

# Turkey Meatballs

**Prep time: 8 minutes**
**Cooking time: 18 minutes**

### Ingredients:
- 2 cups ground turkey
- 3 beaten eggs
- One teaspoon pepper
- One teaspoon oregano
- One tablespoon chopped onion

### Directions:
1. Preheat your air fryer to 390 degrees F.
2. Mix all the ingredients together in a bowl.
3. Form into meatballs by hand.
4. Place in the Air fryer and cook for 18 minutes.
5. Serve with zucchini noodles or another healthy low carb pasta.

# Chicken Burgers

**Prep time: 8 minutes**
**Cooking time: 18 minutes**

### Ingredients:
- 2 cups ground chicken
- 3 beaten eggs
- One teaspoon pepper
- One teaspoon thyme
- One tablespoon chopped garlic

### Directions:
1. Preheat your air fryer to 390 degrees F.
2. Combine the ingredients in a mixing bowl. Stir well by hand or use a hand mixer.
3. Form flat patties with your hands.
4. Place the burgers in the Air fryer and cook for 18 minutes.
5. Serve with salad or gluten free, low carb bread.

# Chicken Zucchini Bites

**Prep time: 15 minutes**
**Cooking time: 25 minutes**

**Ingredients:**
- 2 cups cooked chicken
- 2 cups shredded (grated with cheese grater) zucchini
- ½ cup cream cheese
- One cup chickpea flour, combined with
- 2 tbsp olive oil
- ¼ tsp pepper

**Directions:**
1. Preheat your air fryer to 390 degrees F.
2. In a medium sized bowl, combine the chicken, cream cheese and zucchini.
3. Use your hands to form bite-sized balls.
4. Place the olive oil in a dish and roll the balls in the oil.
5. Roll the balls in the chickpea flour to coat well.
6. Fry in the air fryer for 25 minutes.
7. Serve with barbeque sauce and salad.

# Broccoli Turkey Swiss Balls

**Prep time: 15 minutes**
**Cooking time: 25 minutes**

**Ingredients:**
- 2 cups cooked turkey
- One cup chopped, steamed broccoli heads
- One cup shredded swiss cheese
- One teaspoon black pepper
- One teaspoon garlic powder
- 2 tablespoons olive oil
- One cup almond flour

**Directions:**
1. Preheat your air fryer to 390 degrees F.
2. In a medium sized bowl, combine the turkey, broccoli, swiss cheese, pepper and garlic. Stir to combine well or use a hand mixer (electric).
3. Use your hands to form bite-sized balls.
4. Place the olive oil in a dish and roll the balls in the oil.
5. Roll the balls in the almond flour to coat well.
8. Fry in the air fryer for 25 minutes.
9. Serve with ketchup and salad.

# Crispy Chicken Cheese

**Prep time: 15 minutes**
**Cooking time: 30 minutes**

## Ingredients:
- 2 chicken breasts, cut into slices lengthwise
- Fresh mozzarella, cut into slices
- Two cups chickpea flour

## Directions:
1. Preheat your air fryer to 390 degrees F.
2. Place the sliced mozzarella on top of the chicken strips.
3. Roll the chicken and cheese in the chickpea flour.
4. Place in the air fryer and cook for 30 minutes.
5. Serve with salad and your sauce of choice.

# Turkey Rangoons

**Prep time: 15 minutes**
**Cooking time: 25 minutes**

## Ingredients:
- 4 sheets of gluten free or low carb pastry dough or pie crust cut into squares
- One cup cooked turkey, cut into pieces
- Three cups cream cheese
- ¼ teaspoon black pepper
- One egg, beaten

## Directions:
1. Preheat your air fryer to 390 degrees F.
2. Combine the turkey and cream cheese along with the black pepper in a medium sized mixing bowl.
3. Spoon the mixture onto each pastry square.
4. Brush the edges with egg so the edges stick together. Join the edges.
5. Place in the air fryer and allow cooking for 25 minutes.
6. Serve with sweet and sour sauce and salad.

# Chicken Samosas

**Prep time: 15 minutes**
**Cooking time: 25 minutes**

### Ingredients:
- 4 sheets of gluten free or low carb pastry dough or pie crust cut into squares
- ½ cup cooked chicken
- ½ cup cooked green peas
- ½ cup cooked carrots
- ½ cup cooked potatoes, cut into small bits (substitute with celeriac if looking to go low carb)
- ½ cup cream cheese
- ¼ teaspoon black pepper
- ½ teaspoon chili powder
- One teaspoon olive oil
- One egg, beaten

### Directions:
1. Preheat your air fryer to 390 degrees F.
2. Combine the chicken with the peas, carrots, potatoes and cream cheese along with all of the spices and olive oil in a large mixing bowl.
3. Spoon the mixture into each of the pastries.
4. Brush the edges of the pastries with the beaten egg.
5. Pinch the eggs together to form samosas.
6. Cook in the air fryer for 25-30 minutes.
7. Serve as an appetizer or with a salad as a main meal.

# Turkey Springrolls

**Prep time: 15 minutes**
**Cooking time: 25 minutes**

## Ingredients:

- 6 sheets rice "paper"
- One cup cooked turkey, cut into pieces
- ½ cup cup shredded cabbage
- ½ cup shredded carrots
- Two tablespoons olive oil
- 1 teaspoon black pepper
- ½ teaspoon chili powder
- ½ teaspoon garlic powder

## Directions:

1. Preheat your air fryer to 390 degrees F.
2. Combine the turkey, cabbage, carrots, olive oil, black pepper, chili powder and garlic powder in a mixing bowl.
3. Spoon the mixture onto each pastry square.
4. Roll up the rice paper to form egg rolls. (Possibly brush with egg for extra crispiness).
5. Serve with a salad or as an appetizer.

# Chicken Air fryer Dumplings

**Prep time: 15 minutes**
**Cooking time: 25 minutes**

## Ingredients:

- 4 sheets of gluten free or low carb pastry dough or pie crust cut into squares (coconut or turmeric wraps are a great low carb variant)
- ½ cup cooked chicken
- One cup mashed cauliflower
- One cup cream cheese
- One teaspoon chives
- ½ teaspoon black pepper
- One egg, beaten

## Directions:

1. Preheat your air fryer to 390 degrees F.
2. Combine the chicken, cauliflower, cream cheese, chives and pepper in a bowl.
3. Place in the wraps or pastry dough and roll up. Tuck in ends.
4. Brush with egg.
5. Place in air fryer and cook for 25-30 minutes.

Serve with soup or salad.

# Chicken Sticks

**Prep time: 15 minutes**
**Cooking time: 32 minutes**

## Ingredients:
- 2 chicken breasts, cut into strips and placed on skewers
- ½ cup coconut aminos
- One tablespoon apple cider vinegar
- One tablespoon water
- Pinch of sea salt

## Directions:
1. Preheat your air fryer to 390 degrees F.
2. Stir the sea salt in with the coconut aminos and apple cider vinegar. Place the chicken on the skewers on a bowl along with the mixture. Spoon the mixture over the chicken and allow to sit for 10 minutes.
3. Place the skewers in the air fryer and cook for 32 minutes.
4. Serve with salad or soup or as an appetizer.

# Turkey Dill Cranberry Wraps

**Prep time: 8 minutes**
**Cooking time: 25 minutes**

## Ingredients:
- 4 low carb coconut wraps
- 4 slices baked turkey (or 8 slices turkey cold cuts)
- ½ cup cranberry sauce or lingonberry jam
- One cup mashed cauliflower (or potato if not on a low carb diet)
- Two tablespoons mushroom gravy
- One teaspoon dill

## Directions:
1. Preheat your air fryer to 390 degrees F.
2. Place a slice of turkey (or two cold cuts each) on each wrap. Add a bit of cranberry sauce, a spoonful of mashed cauliflower and one half a teaspoon of mushroom gravy. Sprinkle each wrap with dill.
3. Roll up and place in air fryer and cook for 25 minutes.
4. Enjoy as a hearty lunch or dinner.

# Ultimate Chicken Cheese Sandwich

**Prep time: 15 minutes**
**Cooking time: 25 minutes**

### Ingredients:
- 4 slices gluten free or low carb bread (or your choice of bread)
- One cup cooked, shredded chicken
- One cup cream cheese
- One cup shredded pepper jack cheese
- One tomato, sliced
- ¼ teaspoon black pepper

### Directions:
1. Preheat your air fryer to 390 degrees F.
2. Combine cream cheese and chicken in a bowl.
3. Spread on one slice of bread. Top with tomato and sprinkle with pepper. Then top with cheese. Repeat on the remaining slice of bread.
4. Place in the air fryer and cook for 25 minutes.
5. Serve with pickles.

# Pineapple fried chicken

**Prep time: 5 minutes**
**Cooking time: 30 minutes**

### Ingredients:
- 3 boneless breasts of chicken
- One cup pineapple slices
- One cup coconut milk
- One tablespoon black pepper
- One tablespoon corn starch
- One tablespoon garlic powder
- One tablespoon olive oil

### Directions:
1. Preheat your Airfryer to 390 degrees F.
2. In a food processor, combine the pineapple with the coconut milk, black pepper, garlic powder and corn starch. Puree to a smooth sauce.
3. Brush chicken with olive oil. Place in the Air fryer and cook for 10 minutes.
4. Remove and add the sauce in an oven safe dish.
5. Cook for another 20 minutes.

# Turkey cordon bleu

**Prep time: 5 minutes**
**Cooking time: 25 minutes**

## Ingredients:
- 4 slices of turkey breast
- 2 slices of ham
- One cup gruyere or another type of aged cheese
- 2 eggs, beaten
- 2 cups breadcrumbs

## Directions:
1. Preheat your Airfryer to 390 degrees F.
2. Top one of the turkey slices with ham and half of the cheese.
3. Place another slice of turkey on top.
4. Repeat the procedure with the other two turkey slices and the rest of the cheese and ham.
5. Tip one stack first into the egg mixture, and then into the breadcrumbs. Coat well.
6. Repeat
7. Place on a heat safe dish and cook for 25 minutes.

# Chicken bacon cheese weave

**Prep time: 5 minutes**
**Cooking time: 30 minutes**

## Ingredients:
- 3 filets of boneless chicken breasts
- 9 strips of bacon
- 2 cups mozzarella cheese

## Directions:

1. Preheat your Airfryer to 390 degrees F.
2. Cover the tops of each chicken breast with cheese. Distribute evenly.
3. Wrap the chicken and cheese in bacon. Use 3 strips for each piece of chicken.
4. Fry in the Airfryer for 30 minutes.
5. Enjoy with salad or any side dish of your choice from this book.

# Cream cheese Chicken Pastry

**Prep time: 5 minutes**
**Cooking time: 14 minutes**

**Ingredients:**
- 4 sheets of flaky pastry dough (filo works well)
- 2 cups cream cheese
- 2 cups shredded (cooked) chicken
- 2 cloves garlic, chopped finely
- 2 tablespoons olive oil
- One egg, beaten

**Directions:**
1. Preheat your Airfryer to 390 degrees F.
2. In a medium sized mixing bowl, combine the chicken, garlic, cheese, and one tablespoon of olive oil.
3. Spoon some of the mixture onto each pastry. Fold and tuck in the ends. Brush with the egg to make the ends stick.
4. Brush the tops of each pastry with olive oil.
5. Cut small slits into each pastry.
6. Air fry for 14 minutes.

# Chicken tacos

**Prep time: 5 minutes**
**Cooking time: 18 minutes**

## Ingredients:
- 2 cups shredded chicken
- Two tablespoons chili powder
- One tablespoon black pepper
- One tablespoon garlic powder
- One tablespoon paprika
- One teaspoon fenugreek
- One tablespoon olive oil
- 4 taco shells (soft wraps or crunchy)
- One cup shredded lettuce
- One cup spicy cheese (shredded)
- One cup chopped tomatoes
- One cup taco sauce
- One cup sour cream

## Directions:
1. Preheat your Airfryer to 390 degrees F.
2. Combine the chicken with the chili, pepper, garlic, paprika, fenugreek and olive oil.
3. Place on a heat safe dish and cook for 15 minutes.
4. Place in the taco shells and cook for 3 more minutes.
5. Top with the rest of the toppings and enjoy.

# Artichoke Cream Chicken

**Prep time: 5 minutes**
**Cooking time: 30 minutes**

**Ingredients:**
- 3 boneless breasts of chicken
- One cup artichoke hearts
- One cup sour cream
- One tablespoon black pepper
- One tablespoon garlic powder
- One tablespoon olive oil
- One teaspoon chives

**Directions:**
1. Preheat your Airfryer to 390 degrees F.
2. In a food processor, combine the artichokes with the sour cream, black pepper and garlic powder. Puree to a smooth sauce.
3. Brush chicken with olive oil. Place in the Air fryer and cook for 10 minutes.
4. Remove and add the sauce in an oven safe dish.
5. Cook for another 20 minutes.

# Spinach chicken cheese balls

**Prep time: 5 minutes**
**Cooking time: 15 minutes**

**Ingredients:**
- 2 cups shredded chicken breast (pulled chicken)
- 2 cups cream cheese
- One cup frozen and thawed spinach
- 2 cloves garlic, chopped

**Directions:**
1. Preheat your Airfryer to 390 degrees F.
2. Combine all the ingredients in a bowl.
3. Use your hands to form balls.
4. Place on a heat safe dish and cook for 15 minutes.

# Turkey cranberry cream cheese rolls

**Prep time: 5 minutes**
**Cooking time: 10 minutes**

**Ingredients:**
- 4 sheets of rice "paper" (egg roll sheets)
- two eggs, beaten
- 1 cup cream cheese
- One cup cranberry sauce or lingonberry jam
- 1 ⅓ cup turkey, cut into bite-sized pieces
- One tablespoon coconut oil for greasing pan

**Directions:**
1. Preheat your Airfryer to 390 degrees F.
2. Stir together the cream cheese, cranberry sauce and turkey.
3. Dip each rice "paper" in lukewarm water and remove quickly. Spread flat on a clean surface.
4. Distribute the cheese and turkey mix among the rice sheets.
5. Wrap up and fold over the rice rolls.
6. Dip in the egg mix.
7. Place on a greased, heat safe form and cook in the Air fryer for 10 minutes.
8. Serve with sweet and sour sauce or chutney and sour cream as a side or as a snack or small meal.

# Chicken rolls

**Prep time: 5 minutes**
**Cooking time: 10 minutes**

**Ingredients:**
- 4 sheets of rice "paper" (egg roll sheets)
- two eggs, beaten
- 1 cup cream cheese
- ½ cup shredded cabbage
- ½ cup shredded carrots
- 1 ⅓ cup chicken, cut into bite-sized pieces
- One tablespoon coconut oil for greasing pan

**Directions:**
1. Preheat your Airfryer to 390 degrees F.
2. Stir together the cream cheese, chicken, cabbage and carrots.
3. Dip each rice "paper" in lukewarm water and remove quickly. Spread flat on a clean surface.
4. Distribute the chicken mix among the rice sheets.
5. Wrap up and fold over the rice rolls.
6. Dip in the egg mix.
7. Place on a greased, heat safe form and cook in the Air fryer for 10 minutes.
8. Serve with sweet and sour sauce or chutney and sour cream as a side or as a snack or small meal.

# Chicken buckwheat patties with rosemary

**Prep time: 5 minutes**
**Cooking time: 20 minutes**

**Ingredients:**
- 1 ½ cups buckwheat flakes
- two eggs, beaten
- 1 cup cream cheese
- 1 ½ cups chicken, shredded or pulled cooked chicken
- One tablespoon fresh or dried rosemary
- One tablespoon coconut oil for greasing pan

**Directions:**
1. Preheat your Airfryer to 390 degrees F.
2. Combine all of the ingredients except the coconut oil in a mixing bowl.
3. Grease a heat safe pan with the coconut oil.
4. Form patties by forming balls with your hands and then flattening them onto the pan.
5. Cook for 20 minutes.

# Chicken cauliflower pizza

**Prep time: 10 minutes**
**Cooking time: 25 minutes**

## Ingredients:
- 1 head of cauliflower cooked and cut into florets
- two eggs, beaten
- 1 cup cream cheese
- One cup swiss cheese, shredded
- 1 ½ cups chicken, shredded or pulled cooked chicken
- One tablespoon garlic powder
- 2 cups pizza sauce
- One cup pizza cheese

## Directions:
1. Preheat your Airfryer to 390 degrees F.
2. Squeeze the moisture out of the cauliflower florets using a cheesecloth.
3. Combine the cauliflower, eggs, cream cheese, swiss cheese, chicken and garlic powder in a mixing bowl.
4. Spread out onto a pizza pan (covered in parchment paper). Spread flat to form a crust.
5. Fry in the Air fryer for 15 minutes.
6. Remove and top with the pizza sauce and cheese.
7. Cook for another 10 minutes.

# Chicken stuffed potato

**Prep time: 5 minutes**
**Cooking time: 25 minutes**

## Ingredients:
- 2 large potatoes
- 1 cup sour cream
- One tablespoon garlic powder
- One cup pulled chicken
- One cup cheddar cheese

## Directions:
1. Preheat your Airfryer to 390 degrees F.
2. Place the potatoes in the Air fryer. Poke holes in each potato using a fork. Cook for 15 minutes.
3. Mix together the sour cream, garlic, chicken and cheddar cheese in a bowl.
4. Remove the potatoes. And cut a slit down the middle of each one.
5. Remove some of the potato flesh from inside the potato.
6. Mix with the sour cream combo.
7. Place all of the mixture ingredients in each potato. They will be overflowing, so place on a dish or optionally wrap with tin foil.
8. Cook for 10 more minutes.

# Eggplant Chicken Parmigian

**Prep time: 5 minutes**
**Cooking time: 30 minutes**

## Ingredients:
- 3 boneless breasts of chicken
- Two cups tomato sauce
- One eggplant cut into thin slices
- Two cups mozzarella cheese
- One tablespoon olive oil

## Directions:
1. Preheat your Airfryer to 390 degrees F.
2. Stack the chicken with tomato sauce, cheese and eggplant slices on top of one another.
3. Brush the eggplant with olive oil.
4. Cook for 30 minutes.

# Turkey lasagne
**Prep time: 5 minutes**
**Cooking time: 20 minutes**

## Ingredients:
- 4 slices of turkey breast (thicker slices, use leftover thanksgiving turkey if you want)
- Two cups tomato sauce
- Two cups ricotta cheese
- Two cups mozzarella cheese
- 3 zucchinis sliced lengthwise with a mandolin
- One tablespoon olive oil

## Directions:
1. Preheat your Airfryer to 390 degrees F.
2. Grease a heat safe dish with he olive oil.
3. Top with the zucchini, then add a little sauce, then a turkey slice and some mozzarella and then some ricotta. Repeat the process to layer all ingredients until all of the ingredients have been used.
4. Cook for 20 minutes.

# Chicken nachos
**Prep time: 5 minutes**
**Cooking time: 18 minutes**

## Ingredients:
- One cup cooked chicken, cut into bite sized pieces
- A bag of tortilla chips
- Diced tomatoes
- Diced onions
- One tablespoon fresh cilantro
- Two tablespoons sour cream
- Two cups pepper jack cheese

## Directions:
1. Preheat your Airfryer to 390 degrees F.
2. Arrange all the other ingredients onto the tortilla chips.
3. Cook for 18 minutes

# Fried Chicken Noodles

**Prep time: 5 minutes**
**Cooking time: 10 minutes**

## Ingredients:
- One cup cubed, cooked chicken breast
- Three zucchinis, cut into noodle form with a spiralizer or mandolin
- One cup tomato sauce
- One tablespoon parmesan cheese
- Two garlic cloves, chopped
- Two tablespoons olive oil

## Directions:
1. Preheat your Airfryer to 390 degrees F.
2. Combine all the ingredients in a mixing bowl. Make sure the zucchini noodles are well coated.
3. Place in a heat safe container and then place in the Air fryer.
4. Cook for 10 minutes.

---

# Indian Chicken Stuffed Bread

**Prep time: 5 minutes**
**Cooking time: 30 minutes**

## Ingredients:
- Three cups worth of risen bread dough
- ½ cup potatoes, cut into very small cubes
- ½ cup small carrots (also cut into very small cubes)
- ½ cup peas
- One cup coconut curry (coconut milk plus Indian curry mix)

## Directions:
1. Preheat your Airfryer to 390 degrees F.
2. Take the risen bread and use your hands to "dig" (move) the sides out so that you can make space for the stuffing ingredients.
3. Mix the peas, carrots and potatoes with the coconut curry.
4. Stuff the bread with the curry mix.
5. Fold over the top so the stuffing is enclosed.
6. Brush with a bit of olive oil and bake for 30 minutes.

# Spicy Chicken balls
**Prep time: 5 minutes**
**Cooking time: 30 minutes**

## Ingredients:
- One pound ground chicken
- Three eggs
- One tablespoon chili powder
- One tablespoon garlic powder
- One tablespoon black pepper

## Directions:
1. Preheat your Airfryer to 390 degrees F.
2. Combine all the ingredients in a mixing bowl.
3. Form balls using a spoon and/or your hands.
4. Fry the chicken balls on a heat safe dish greased with olive oil.
5. Cook for 30 minutes.

# Stuffed Tomato Chicken
**Prep time: 5 minutes**
**Cooking time: 25 minutes**

## Ingredients:
- 4 slices of chicken breast
- Two cups tomato sauce
- 3 eggs, beaten
- Two cups mozzarella cheese
- 3 cups chickpea flour
- One tablespoon olive oil

## Directions:
1. Preheat your Airfryer to 390 degrees F.
2. Spread cheese and tomato sauce in between two of the chicken slices (to form a sandwich type formation).
3. Dip each "sandwich" first in the egg and then in the chickpea flour.
4. Place on a heat safe, greased with olive oil dish.
5. Cook in the Air fryer for 25 minutes.

# Chicken Stuffed Bacon

**Prep time: 5 minutes**
**Cooking time: 25 minutes**

**Ingredients:**
- 4 slices of chicken breast
- 4 slices bacon
- 3 eggs, beaten
- Two cups cream cheese
- 3 cups chickpea flour
- One tablespoon olive oil

**Directions:**
1. Preheat your Airfryer to 390 degrees F.
2. Spread cheese and place bacon between two of the chicken slices (to form a sandwich type formation).
3. Dip each "sandwich" first in the egg and then in the chickpea flour.
4. Place on a heat safe, greased with olive oil dish.
5. Cook in the Air fryer for 25 minutes.

# Meat

## Beef Beet Burgers
**Prep time: 8 minutes**
**Cooking time: 18 minutes**

### Ingredients:
- 1 1/2 cups ground beef
- 1/2 cup shredded beets
- 3 beaten eggs
- One teaspoon pepper
- One teaspoon thyme
- One tablespoon chopped garlic

### Directions:
1. Preheat your air fryer to 390 degrees F.
2. Combine the ingredients in a mixing bowl. Stir well by hand or use a hand mixer.
3. Form flat patties with your hands.
4. Place the burgers in the Air fryer and cook for 18 minutes.
5. Serve with salad or gluten free, low carb bread.

## Stuffed Mushrooms with bacon
**Prep time: 15 minutes**
**Cooking time: 15 minutes**

### Ingredients:
- 2 bacon (rashers)
- half of an onion
- half of a capsicum
- 1 carrot
- 24 mushrooms (medium sized)
- 1 cup grated cheese
- 1/2 cup sour cream

### Directions:
1. Preheat your air fryer to 350 degrees F.
2. Dice onion, bacon, carrot, mushroom stems and capsicum.
3. Fry vegetables and bacon in a pan until they become soft.
4. Add in cheese and sour cream. Continue to heat until all products mixed well.
5. Add stuffing into each mushroom cap
6. Put the mushrooms into air fryer basket.
7. Cook for 8-10 minutes.

# Carrot Venison Meatballs

**Prep time: 10 minutes**
**Cooking time: 16 minutes**

Ingredients:
- 2 cups ground venison
- 1 cup carrots
- 3 beaten eggs
- One teaspoon pepper
- One teaspoon oregano
- One tablespoon chopped garlic

Directions:
1. Preheat your air fryer to 390 degrees F.
2. Combine the ingredients in a mixing bowl. Stir well by hand or use a hand mixer.
3. Form meatballs with your hands.
4. Place the meatballs in the Air fryer and cook for 16 minutes.
5. Serve with salad or gluten free, low carb bread.

# Swedish meatballs

**Prep time: 5 minutes**
**Cooking time: 18 minutes**

Ingredients:
- Half a pound of ground beef or ground pork
- 1 egg
- A bit of salt and pepper

Directions:
1. Preheat the Airfryer to 360 degrees F.
2. Combine the meat, egg and salt and pepper in a bowl.
3. Form the mixture into meatballs.
4. Place the meatballs in the Airfryer and cook for 18 minutes.
5. Check to make sure the meatballs are cooked through by cutting one open. If the meat has remained somewhat red or pink, then cook for another three minutes and check once more.
6. Serve with parsnip fries or mashed potatoes and a side of lingonberry jam.

# Meatballs (spaghetti and meatballs)
**Prep time: 10 minutes**
**Cooking time: 18 minutes**

**Ingredients**:
- Half a pound of ground beef
- 1 egg
- Italian seasoning (oregano, chopped garlic, pepper, salt)
- Prepared spaghetti and tomato sauce

**Directions:**
1. Preheat the Airfryer to 360 degrees F.
2. In a mixing bowl, combine the ground beef, the egg and the seasoning blend. Stir well.
3. Form the mixture into meatballs.
4. Place the meatballs in the Airfryer basket.
5. Cook for 18 minutes, checking periodically. Make sure the meatballs are cooked through to the center by cutting one open. If it is still pinkish, cook for another 3 minutes and check again.
6. Serve with noodles, sauce and a salad

# Spicy Steak Sticks
**Prep time: 8 minutes**
**Cooking time: 18 minutes**

**Ingredients:**
- One pound steak, cut into strips
- 2 tablespoons of olive oil
- One teaspoon coconut sugar

**Special tools:**
- wooden skewers for the steak sticks

**Directions:**
1. Preheat your air fryer to 390 degrees F.
2. Mix the olive oil and coconut sugar.
3. Skewer the steak strips with the skewers.
4. Brush with the olive oil and coconut sugar.
5. Place in the Airfryer and cook for 18 minutes.

# Bacon Cheese Balls

**Prep time: 8 minutes**
**Cooking time: 15 minutes**

## Ingredients:
- One pound bacon, smashed to bacon bits
- 2 cups shredded pepper jack cheese
- 2 beaten eggs
- One cup almond flour
- One teaspoon pepper
- One teaspoon oregano
- One tablespoon chopped garlic

## Directions:
1. Preheat your air fryer to 390 degrees F.
2. Combine the bacon bits, cheese, spices and egg in a bowl. Use your hands to distribute the ingredients well as it will be a thick mixture.
3. Roll each ball in the almond meal.
4. Place in the Air fryer and cook for 15 minutes.

# Pork Balls

**Prep time: 5 minutes**
**Cooking time: 14 minutes**

## Ingredients:
- 10.5 oz minced pork
- 2 oz onion (peeled and diced)
- 1 tsp mustard
- 1 tsp garlic puree
- 1 tbsp cheddar cheese (grated)
- handful fresh basil
- salt
- pepper

## Directions:
1. Preheat your air fryer to 390 degrees F.
2. Peel and dice onion.
3. Chop basil into small pieces.
4. In a bowl mix mince, cheese, mustard, garlic puree, basil and onion. Salt and pepper it and mix again.
5. Form into balls.
6. Put balls in air fryer basket.
7. Cook for 12-14 minutes.

# Pork Chop

**Prep time: 5 minutes**
**Cooking time: 15 minutes**

## Ingredients:
- 2 pcs pork chop
- 1 tbsp plain flour
- 1 egg
- 2 tsp olive oil
- 1/2 cup bread crumbs
- salt
- black pepper

## Directions:
1. Preheat your air fryer to 390 degrees F.
2. Salt and pepper pork chop.
3. In a bowl beat the egg.
4. In another bowl mix bread crumbs with oil.
5. Coat meat with a layer of flour on both sides.
6. Dip pork chop in the beaten egg.
7. Coat it with bread crumbs.
8. Put pork chop in air fryer basket.
9. Cook for 8-10 minutes.
10. Turn meat and cook for additional 5 minutes

# Lamb Burgers

**Prep time: 8 minutes**
**Cooking time: 18 minutes**

## Ingredients:
- 2 cups ground lamb meat
- 3 beaten eggs
- One teaspoon pepper
- One teaspoon ground caraway
- One teaspoon oregano
- One tablespoon chopped garlic

## Directions:
1. Preheat your air fryer to 390 degrees F.
2. Combine the ingredients in a mixing bowl. Stir well by hand or use a hand mixer.
3. Form flat patties with your hands.
4. Place the burgers in the Air fryer and cook for 18 minutes.
5. Serve with salad or gluten free, low carb bread.

# Steak Enchiladas (low carb)
Prep time: 8 minutes
Cooking time: 12 minutes

## Ingredients:
- 2 cups steak strips (pre-fried in Air-fryer for 15 minutes)
- 5 coconut wraps (low carb and gluten free)
- One teaspoon garlic powder
- One teaspoon chili powder
- One chopped green bell pepper
- One cup shredded spicy cheese
- One chopped onion

## Directions:
1. Preheat your air fryer to 390 °F.
2. Place the steak, pepper, cheese and onion in the coconut wraps. Distribute the ingredients evenly.
3. Sprinkle with garlic powder and chili powder.
4. Wrap up the enchiladas.
5. Place in the Airfryer and cook for 12 minutes. Top with salsa.

# Schnitzel Parmigiana
Prep time: 10 minutes
Cooking time: 20 minutes

## Ingredients:
- 1 schnitzel (previously crumbed)
- 3 tbsp pasta sauce (jarred)
- 1/3 cup grated cheese

## Directions:
1. Preheat your air fryer to 350 degrees F.
2. Put the schnitzel into air fryer basket.
3. Cook for 15 minutes.
4. Serve pasta sauce over hot schnitzel.
5. Sprinkle grated cheese on schnitzel.
6. Cook for additional 5 minutes.

# Bacon Beef Taco Rolls

**Prep time: 8 minutes**
**Cooking time: 15 minutes**

### Ingredients:
- 2 cups ground beef, browned and cooked with taco spices (chilli, garlic powder, black pepper)
- 1/2 cup bacon bits
- One cup shredded jack cheese
- One cup tomato salsa
- 4 turmeric coconut wraps (gluten free, low carb)

### Directions:
7. Preheat your air fryer to 390 °F.
8. Place the ground beef, bacon bits, cheese and salsa in the coconut wraps and roll up the wraps.
9. Place the taco wraps in the Air fryer and cook for 15 minutes.

# Low Carb Schnitzel

**Prep time: 8 minutes**
**Cooking time: 20 minutes**

### Ingredients:
- 3 veal steaks
- 1 beaten egg
- Two cups almond meal
- One teaspoon pepper

### Directions:
1. Preheat your air fryer to 390 °F.
2. Place almond meal and pepper in a bowl together.
3. Put one of the steaks into the egg mixture, and then transfer to the almond meal. Coat well.
4. Place in the Air fryer and cook for 20 minutes or until the schnitzel is fully cooked.

# Cheesy Pork Filets

**Prep time: 8 minutes**
**Cooking time: 20 minutes**

## Ingredients:
- 3 pork filets
- 1 beaten egg
- Two cups buckwheat flour
- 3 slices swiss cheese
- One teaspoon pepper

## Directions:
1. Preheat your air fryer to 390 °F.
2. Coat the pork filets in egg. Place a slice of cheese on top of each filet. Brush a little more egg on top of each cheese slice.
3. Coat the filets by dipping them into the buckwheat flour.
4. Cook in the Air fryer for 20 minutes or until thoroughly cooked.

# Spicy Venison Burgers

**Prep time: 8 minutes**
**Cooking time: 22 minutes**

## Ingredients:
- 2 cups ground venison (deer) meat
- 3 beaten eggs
- One tablespoon pepper
- One teaspoon ginger powder
- One tablespoon chili pepper
- One teaspoon crushed red pepper
- One tablespoon chopped garlic

## Directions:
1. Preheat your air fryer to 390 degrees F.
2. Combine the ingredients in a mixing bowl. Stir well by hand or use a hand mixer.
3. Form flat patties with your hands.
4. Place the burgers in the Air fryer and cook for 18 minutes.
5. Serve with salad or gluten free, low carb bread.

# Beef Springrolls

**Prep time: 15 minutes**
**Cooking time: 25 minutes**

**Ingredients:**
- 6 sheets rice "paper"
- One cup steak strips
- ½ cup cup shredded purple cabbage
- ½ cup shredded carrots
- Two tablespoons olive oil
- One tablespoon tamari or your choice of soy sauce
- 1 teaspoon black pepper
- ½ teaspoon garlic powder

**Directions:**
1. Preheat your air fryer to 390 degrees F.
2. Combine the steak strips, cabbage, carrots, olive oil, black pepper, soy sauce and garlic powder in a mixing bowl.
3. Spoon the mixture onto each pastry square.
4. Roll up the rice paper to form egg rolls. (Possibly brush with egg for extra crispiness).
5. Serve with a salad or as an appetizer.

# Steak Rolls

**Prep time: 15 minutes**
**Cooking time: 25 minutes**

**Ingredients:**
- 4 low carb wraps (coconut wraps or turmeric wraps)
- 4 slices of thin steak (leftovers can work great, otherwise pastrami and roast beef are good choices)
- Two tablespoons sour cream
- One green pepper, cut into bits
- One yellow onion, chopped
- One pinch sea salt

**Directions:**
1. Preheat your air fryer to 390 degrees F.
2. Spread a layer of sour cream onto each wrap.
3. Add the pepper, onion and sea salt and finally top with each piece of steak.
4. Roll up and place in the air fryer and cook for 25 minutes.
5. Cut into smaller rolls to serve as appetizers or enjoy as lunch wraps.

# Spicy Meatballs

**Prep time: 15 minutes**
**Cooking time: 32 minutes**

## Ingredients:
- Two cups ground beef
- One tablespoon chili
- Three eggs
- One tablespoon black pepper
- One tablespoon garlic powder

## Directions:
1. Preheat your air fryer to 390 degrees F.
2. Combine the ground beef, eggs and spices in a bowl. Stir well.
3. Form meatballs with the hands or two spoons.
4. Place the meatballs in the air fryer and cook for 32 minutes.
5. Serve with spaghetti and meatballs (a great low carn version is with zucchini noodles).

# Ham and Cheese Deluxe

**Prep time: 15 minutes**
**Cooking time: 25 minutes**

## Ingredients:
- 4 slices low carb bread or bread of your choice
- 4 slices of ham
- 4 slices cheddar or swiss cheese
- One tablespoon honey
- One tablespoon tahini

## Directions:
1. Preheat your air fryer to 390 degrees F.
2. Combine the honey and tahini in a small dish.
3. Spoon the dressing onto the bread.
4. Place two slices of ham and two slices of cheese between two slices of bread.
5. Place each sandwich in the air fryer and cook for 25 minutes.
6. Serve with salad or soup for a hearty lunch.

# Pork Melt

**Prep time: 15 minutes**
**Cooking time: 25 minutes**

## Ingredients:
- 4 slices low carb bread or bread of your choice
- 2 pork steaks (pre cooked)
- 2 slices sharp cheddar
- One tablespoon barbeque sauce

## Directions:
1. Preheat your air fryer to 390 degrees F.
2. Spread the barbeque sauce onto the bread.
3. Place a pork steak on top and then top that with cheddar cheese.
4. Put the other slice of bread on top.
5. Place in the air fryer and cook for 25 minutes.

# Italian Beef Roast

**Prep time: 15 minutes**
**Cooking time: 25 minutes**

## Ingredients:
- 4 slices thickly sliced roast beef
- 2 tablespoons marinara sauce (your favorite home made or store bought sauce)
- One cup sliced fresh mozzarella
- 4 leaves basil, torn into bits

## Directions:
1. Preheat your air fryer to 390 degrees F.
2. Spread a tablespoon of sauce onto two of the slices.
3. Add the basil and top with the mozzarella.
4. Top with another slice of roast beef so that you now have two "sandwiches".
5. Place in the air fryer and cook for 25 minutes.
6. Serve with salad and zucchini noodles.

# Pastrami Roll Ups

**Prep time: 8 minutes**
**Cooking time: 15 minutes**

### Ingredients:
- 6 slices pastrami
- Three tablespoons cream cheese
- One cup shredded swiss cheese
- One sliced tomato

### Directions:
1. Preheat your air fryer to 390 degrees F.
2. On each pastrami slice, spread cream cheese, top with tomato and swiss cheese. Roll each slice up.
3. Place in the air fryer and cook for 15 minutes.
4. Serve with a salad for a good low carb meal.

# Fried Soft Tacos

**Prep time: 15 minutes**
**Cooking time: 15 minutes**

### Ingredients:
- 4 low carb wraps or taco tortillas
- Two cups fried ground beef with taco spices (chili, curcumin, black pepper, paprika powder, garlic powder and a tablespoon of tomato sauce should be used to prepare the taco meat)
- Two cups pepper jack or other spicy cheese
- One cup chopped tomatoes
- Two tablespoons sour cream
- One cup lettuce (to top with after)
- Three tablespoons taco sauce

### Directions:
1. Preheat your air fryer to 390 degrees F.
2. Place a spoonful of the meat, cheese, tomatoes and taco sauce in the center of a wrap.
3. Fold the wraps and place in the air fryer.
4. Cook for 15 minutes. Remove and top with lettuce. Double up ingredients to serve a larger group.

# Meaty Filled Tomatoes

**Prep time: 15 minutes**
**Cooking time: 20 minutes**

## Ingredients:
- Two cups ground beef
- One cup tomato sauce
- ¼ teaspoon garlic powder
- ¼ teaspoon black pepper
- 6 large beefsteak tomatoes, sliced at the top with most of the contents removed
- One tablespoon chopped onion

## Directions:
1. Preheat your air fryer to 390 degrees F.
2. Combine the ground beef, tomato sauce, onion, garlic and pepper in a medium sized bowl.
3. Spoon the mixture into the hollowed out beefsteak tomatoes.
4. Cook in the air fryer for 20 minutes.

# Beef Filled Eggplant

**Prep time: 15 minutes**
**Cooking time: 25 minutes**

## Ingredients:
- One cup ground beef
- One cup cream cheese
- ¼ teaspoon garlic powder
- ¼ teaspoon black pepper
- One cup chopped red bell pepper
- One cup swiss cheese
- One eggplant, cut in half with contents partially removed

## Directions:
1. Preheat your air fryer to 390 degrees F.
2. Combine the ground beef, cream cheese, red pepper, garlic and black pepper in a medium sized bowl.
3. Spoon the mixture into the hollowed out eggplant halves.
4. Top with the swiss cheese.
5. Cook in the air fryer for 25 minutes.

# Bacon Burger Wrap

**Prep time: 5 minutes**
**Cooking time: 25 minutes**

## Ingredients:
- 4 burger patties
- 12 slices of bacon
- 2 cups cream cheese

## Directions:

1. Preheat your Airfryer to 390 degrees F.
2. Place a dollop of cream cheese on each of the burger patties.
3. Wrap each one with 3 slices of bacon.
4. Place in the Air fryer and cook for 25 minutes.

# Hamburger stuffed sweet potato

**Prep time: 5 minutes**
**Cooking time: 25 minutes**

## Ingredients:
- 2 large sweet potatoes
- 1 cup sour cream
- One tablespoon garlic powder
- One cup cooked hamburger meat
- One cup cheddar cheese

## Directions:
1. Preheat your Airfryer to 390 degrees F.
2. Peel the sweet potatoes.
3. Place the potatoes in the Air fryer. Poke holes in each potato using a fork. Cook for 15 minutes.
4. Mix together the sour cream, garlic, hamburger and cheddar cheese in a bowl.
5. Remove the potatoes. And cut a slit down the middle of each one.
6. Remove some of the potato flesh from inside the potato.
7. Mix with the sour cream combo.
8. Place all of the mixture ingredients in each potato. They will be overflowing, so place on a dish or optionally wrap with tin foil.
9. Cook for 10 more minutes.

# Zucchini Ham Wraps

**Prep time: 5 minutes**
**Cooking time: 15 minutes**

## Ingredients:
- 4 slices of ham
- 2 large zucchinis, sliced lengthwise with a mandolin
- One tablespoon mustard
- One cup cream cheese

## Directions:
1. Preheat your Airfryer to 390 degrees F.
2. In a bowl, mix together the mustard and cream cheese.
3. Spread on the slices of ham. Place slices of zucchini on top and roll up.
4. Brush with olive oil and fry for 15 minutes.

# Steak Cheese Bombs

**Prep time: 5 minutes**
**Cooking time: 15 minutes**

## Ingredients:
- 4 slices of pastrami or sliced steak
- One cup swiss cheese
- One cup cream cheese

## Directions:
1. Preheat your Airfryer to 390 degrees F.
2. In a bowl, mix together the  swiss and cream cheese.
3. Spread on the slices of pastrami.
4. Brush with olive oil and fry for 15 minutes.

# Pastrami Onion Wraps

**Prep time: 5 minutes**
**Cooking time: 15 minutes**

**Ingredients:**
- 8 slices pastrami
- 4 wraps (or soft tortillas)
- One onion, sliced into rings
- One cup cream cheese
- One cup cheddar cheese
- One tablespoon garlic powder
- One tomato, sliced

**Directions:**
1. Preheat your Airfryer to 390 degrees F.
2. Mix the cream cheese, cheddar cheese and garlic powder. Spread onto each wrap.
3. Place two slices of pastrami onto each wrap. Add the tomato and onion. Roll up.
4. Fry for 15 minutes.

# Hamburger Egg Rolls

**Prep time: 5 minutes**
**Cooking time: 10 minutes**

**Ingredients:**
- 5 sheets of rice "paper" (egg roll sheets)
- two eggs, beaten
- One tablespoon onion powder
- One tablespoon garlic powder
- 1 ½ cups browned ground beef (fried in Airfryer or over the stovetop)
- ½ cup herbed cream cheese
- Two tablespoons chili powder
- ½ cup shredded carrots.
- ½ cup shredded cabbage

**Directions:**
1. Preheat your Airfryer to 390 degrees F.
2. Mix the cheese, carrots, beef, chili, cabbage and the onion and garlic powder.
3. Dip each rice "paper" in lukewarm water and remove quickly. Spread flat on a clean surface.
4. Distribute the beef mix evenly among the rice sheets.
5. Wrap up and fold over the rice rolls.
6. Dip in the egg mix.
7. Place on a greased, heat safe form and cook in the Air fryer for 10 minutes.

# Cheesy Meatballs
**Prep time: 5 minutes**
**Cooking time: 30 minutes**

## Ingredients:
- One pound ground beef
- Three eggs
- One cup cream cheese
- One cup mozzarella cheese
- One tablespoon chili powder
- One tablespoon garlic powder
- One tablespoon black pepper

## Directions:

1. Preheat your Airfryer to 390 degrees F.
2. Combine all the ingredients in a mixing bowl.
3. Form balls using a spoon and/or your hands.
4. Fry the meatballs on a heat safe dish greased with olive oil.
5. Cook for 30 minutes.

# Hamburger Cream Cheese Spinach Fried balls
**Prep time: 5 minutes**
**Cooking time: 30 minutes**

## Ingredients:
- One pound ground beef
- Three eggs
- One cup cream cheese
- One cup swiss cheese
- One cup frozen and thawed spinach
- One tablespoon garlic powder
- One tablespoon black pepper

## Directions:
1. Preheat your Airfryer to 390 degrees F.
2. Combine all the ingredients in a mixing bowl.
3. Form balls using a spoon and/or your hands.
4. Fry the meatballs on a heat safe dish greased with olive oil.
5. Cook for 30 minutes.

# Cauliflower Hamburger Pizza

Prep time: 10 minutes
Cooking time: 25 minutes

**Ingredients:**
- 1 head of cauliflower cooked and cut into florets
- two eggs, beaten
- 1 cup cream cheese
- One cup swiss cheese, shredded
- One cup cooked hamburger meat
- One onion, diced
- One tablespoon onion powder
- One tablespoon garlic powder
- 2 cups pizza sauce
- One cup pizza cheese

**Directions:**
1. Preheat your Airfryer to 390 degrees F.
2. Squeeze the moisture out of the cauliflower florets using cheesecloth.
3. Combine the cauliflower, eggs, cream cheese, Swiss cheese, onion and garlic powder in a mixing bowl.
4. Spread out onto a pizza pan (covered in parchment paper). Spread flat to form a crust.
5. Fry in the Air fryer for 15 minutes.
6. Remove and top with the pizza sauce and cheese as well as the hamburger meat
7. Cook for another 10 minutes.

# Sour Cream Onion Steaks

Prep time: 5 minutes
Cooking time: 25 minutes

**Ingredients:**
- 2 steak filet
- One cup sour cream
- One tablespoon onion powder
- One onion, cut into rings

**Directions:**
1. Preheat your Airfryer to 390 degrees F.
2. Mix together the onion powder, sour cream and onion rings.
3. Place the steaks in the Airfryer and cook for 15 minutes.
4. Add the auce and cook for another 10 minutes.

# Double Cheese Burrito

**Prep time: 10 minutes**
**Cooking time: 25 minutes**

## Ingredients:
- 2 cups steak strips
- One cup taco sauce
- One cup cream cheese
- 4 tortilla wraps
- One cup pepper jack cheese
- One tomato, diced
- One tablespoon fresh cilantro, diced

## Directions:
1. Preheat your Airfryer to 390 degrees F.
2. Mix together the steak, taco sauce, cream cheese, pepper jack, tomato and cilantro.
3. Spoon out onto each of the tortillas. Wrap up the tortillas.
4. Fry for 25 minutes.

# Cheesy Cabbage Steak Wraps

**Prep time: 10 minutes**
**Cooking time: 25 minutes**

## Ingredients:
- 2 cups steak strips
- One cup shredded cabbage
- One cup cream cheese
- 4 tortilla wraps
- One cup swiss cheese
- One tablespoon black pepper
- One pinch salt

## Directions:
1. Preheat your Airfryer to 390 degrees F.
2. Mix together the steak, cabbage, cream cheese,swiss, salt and pepper.
3. Spoon out onto each of the tortillas. Wrap up the tortillas.
4. Fry for 25 minutes.

# Fried Bolognese Bread

**Prep time: 10 minutes**
**Cooking time: 15 minutes**

## Ingredients:
- 2 cups ground beef, already fried and browned
- Two cups spaghetti sauce
- 2 baguettes, sliced lengthwise
- One cup cream cheese

## Directions:
1. Preheat your Airfryer to 390 degrees F.
2. Mix all of the ingredients except the bread.
3. Spread the beef mix onto the bread.
4. Fry for 15 minutes.

# Pork Cheddar Broccoli Balls

**Prep time: 5 minutes**
**Cooking time: 30 minutes**

## Ingredients:
- One pound ground pork
- Three eggs
- One cup cream cheese
- One cup cheddar cheese
- One cup frozen and thawed broccoli in small florets
- One tablespoon garlic powder
- One tablespoon onion powder
- One tablespoon black pepper

## Directions:
1. Preheat your Airfryer to 390 degrees F.
2. Combine all the ingredients in a mixing bowl.
3. Form balls using a spoon and/or your hands.
4. Fry the meatballs on a heat safe dish greased with olive oil.
5. Cook for 30 minutes.

# Pepperoni Eggplant Pizzas

**Prep time: 5 minutes**
**Cooking time: 25 minutes**

## Ingredients:
- Pizza crust (self made from one of the cauliflower recipes in this book or any other pizza crust recipe)
- Two cups pizza sauce
- Two cups pizza cheese (mozzarella, shredded or fresh)
- One eggplant, cut into bite-sized pieces
- Pepperonis

## Directions:
1. Preheat your Airfryer to 390 degrees F.
2. Spread out the pizza crust.
3. Top with pizza sauce, then pizza cheese and the eggplant and pepperoni.
4. Cook for 25 minutes.

# Pastrami Bacon Rolls

**Prep time: 5 minutes**
**Cooking time: 15 minutes**

## Ingredients:
- 6 slices of pastrami
- One cup cream cheese
- One cup mashed potatoes
- One egg
- Two cups bacon bits

## Directions:
1. Preheat your Airfryer to 390 degrees F.
2. Combine the cream cheese, mashed potatoes, egg and bacon.
3. Spoon a bit into each slice of pastrami. Roll up.
4. Cook for 15 minutes.

# Hot salad with bacon

**Prep time: 5 minutes**
**Cooking time: 30 minutes**

## Ingredients:
- Two cups bacon bits
- One cup shredded carrots
- One cup shredded parsnip
- One cup shredded purple cabbage
- One onion, chopped
- One tomato, sliced

## Directions:
1. Preheat your Airfryer to 390 degrees F.
2. Combine all the ingredients in a mixing bowl.
3. Place in a heat safe dish and cook for 15 minutes.

# Beef and Potato

**Prep time: 5 minutes**
**Cooking time: 20 minutes**

## Ingredients:
- One pound ground beef, fried and browned
- Three cups mashed potatoes
- Two eggs
- Two tablespoons garlic powder
- One cup sour cream
- One pinch salt
- One tablespoon black pepper

## Directions:
1. Preheat your Airfryer to 390 degrees F.
2. Combine all the ingredients in a mixing bowl.
3. Place in a heat safe dish and cook for 20 minutes.

# Pesto beef

**Prep time: 5 minutes**
**Cooking time: 30 minutes**

## Ingredients:
- One large beef steak, brushed with olive oil
- One cup pesto

## Directions:
1. Preheat your Airfryer to 390 degrees F.
2. Fry the steak for 15 minutes. Remove from heat.
3. Top with the pesto and return to the Airfryer.
4. Cook for another five minutes.

# Steak strips curry

**Prep time: 5 minutes**
**Cooking time: 20 minutes**

## Ingredients:
- Two cups cooked steak strips
- Two cups coconut milk
- Three tablespoons curry mix (or make your own with chili powder, turmeric, fenugreek)
- One tablespoon garlic powder
- One tablespoon black pepper
- One tomato, chopped
- One cup spinach
- One cup broccoli

## Directions:
1. Preheat your Airfryer to 390 degrees F.
2. Combine all the ingredients in a mixing bowl.
3. Place in a heat safe dish. Cook for 20 minutes.
4. Serve over rice.

# Vegetarian

## Crispy Zucchini Spirals
**Prep time: 10 minutes**
**Cooking time: 15 minutes**

**Ingredients:**
- Three spiralized whole zucchinis (cut into noodles with either a mandolin or spiralizer)
- One tablespoon olive oil
- ¼ teaspoon garlic powder
- ¼ teaspoon black pepper
- One tomato, chopped into bits

**Directions:**
1. Preheat your air fryer to 390 degrees F.
2. Combine the zucchini noodles with the olive oil, garlic, pepper and tomato.
3. Place in the air fryer and cook for 15 minutes. Serve with a cream sauce.

## Crispy Carrot Noodles
**Prep time: 10 minutes**
**Cooking time: 15 minutes**

**Ingredients:**
- Five spiralized whole carrots(cut into noodles with either a mandolin or spiralizer)
- One tablespoon olive oil
- ¼ teaspoon garlic powder
- ¼ teaspoon black pepper
- One tablespoon raisins
- Two tablespoons tahini

**Directions:**
1. Preheat your air fryer to 390 degrees F.
2. Combine the carrot noodles with the olive oil, garlic, pepper, raisins and tahini. Take extra care to make sure the tahini is evenly combined with the other ingredients.

# Vegetarian Egg Rolls

**Prep time: 15 minutes**
**Cooking time: 25 minutes**

**Ingredients:**
- 6 sheets rice "paper"
- One cup tofu or seitan
- ½ cup shredded purple cabbage
- ½ cup shredded carrots
- Two tablespoons olive oil
- One tablespoon tamari or your choice of soy sauce
- 1 teaspoon black pepper
- ½ teaspoon garlic powder

**Directions:**
1. Preheat your air fryer to 390 degrees F.
2. Combine the tofu, cabbage, carrots, olive oil, black pepper, soy sauce and garlic powder in a mixing bowl.
3. Spoon the mixture onto each pastry square.
4. Roll up the rice paper to form egg rolls. (Possibly brush with egg for extra crispiness).
5. Serve with a salad or as an appetizer along with sweet and sour sauce.

# Vegetarian Schnitzel

**Prep time: 15 minutes**
**Cooking time: 25 minutes**

**Ingredients:**
- One large celeriac (celery root), sliced to about ¼ inch thick
- One egg, beaten
- Two cups almond flour
- ¼ teaspoon black pepper
- ¼ teaspoon garlic powder

**Directions:**
1. Preheat your air fryer to 390 degrees F.
2. Combine the almond flour with the pepper and garlic powder.
3. Place the celeriac in the egg mixture, then turn.
4. Transfer to the almond flour mixture and turn the "schnitzel". Be sure to coat well.
5. Cook in the air fryer for 25 minutes. Serve with a mushroom sauce and potato salad or green salad.

# Air fryer Eggplant Parmesan

**Prep time: 15 minutes**
**Cooking time: 25 minutes**

## Ingredients:
- One eggplant, cut into slices
- One egg, beaten
- Two cups almond flour
- ¼ teaspoon black pepper
- ¼ teaspoon garlic powder
- Two cups of homemade or other favorite marinara sauce
- Two cups mozzarella cheese, shredded or fresh and cut into slices

## Directions:
1. Preheat your air fryer to 390 degrees F.
2. Combine the almond flour with the pepper and garlic powder.
3. Place the eggplant in the egg mixture, then turn.
4. Transfer to the almond flour mixture and turn eggplant slices.
5. Top with the sauce and mozzarella.
6. Cook in the air fryer for 25 minutes. Serve with salad and or bread.

# Rosemary Cauliflower

**Prep time: 15 minutes**
**Cooking time: 25 minutes**

## Ingredients:
- One large head of cauliflower, torn into smaller bits
- Two eggs, beaten
- ¼ teaspoon black pepper
- ¼ teaspoon garlic powder
- ¼ teaspoon rosemary (dried or fresh)

## Directions:
1. Preheat your air fryer to 390 degrees F.
2. Place the spices in with the beaten egg and stir to combine.
3. Then transfer the cauliflower to the egg mixture. Coat well.
4. Place the cauliflower in the air fryer and cook for 25 minutes.
5. Serve with a sour cream dip and salad.

# Beet Burgers
**Prep time: 15 minutes**
**Cooking time: 25 minutes**

### Ingredients:
- Two cups shredded red beets
- One cup chickpea flour
- One egg, beaten
- ¼ teaspoon black pepper
- ¼ teaspoon garlic powder

### Directions:
1. Preheat your air fryer to 390 degrees F.
2. Combine the chickpea flour with the pepper and garlic powder.
3. Then stir in the beets and the egg. Use a large wooden spoon or your hands to combine well.
4. Use your hands to form burger patties.
5. Place the beet burgers in the air fryer and cook for 25 minutes.
6. Serve with low carb or gluten free bread, mayonnaise and pickles and salad.

# Peanut Carrot Burgers
**Prep time: 15 minutes**
**Cooking time: 25 minutes**

### Ingredients:
- Two cups shredded carrots
- One cup peanut flour
- One egg, beaten
- ¼ teaspoon black pepper
- ¼ teaspoon garlic powder

### Directions:
1. Preheat your air fryer to 390 degrees F.
2. Combine the peanut flour with the pepper and garlic powder.
3. Then stir in the carrots and the egg. Use a large wooden spoon or your hands to combine well.
4. Use your hands to form burger patties.
5. Place the carrot burgers in the air fryer and cook for 25 minutes.
6. Serve with low carb or gluten free bread, mayonnaise and pickles and salad.

# Lemon Lentil Burgers

Prep time: 15 minutes
Cooking time: 25 minutes

Ingredients:
- Two cups cooked green lentils
- Two tablespoons lemon juice
- One cup chickpea flour
- One egg, beaten
- ¼ teaspoon black pepper
- ¼ teaspoon garlic powder

Directions:
1. Preheat your air fryer to 390 degrees F.
2. Place all of the ingredients in a food processor and pulse for a few seconds.
3. Use your hands to form burger patties.
4. Place in the air fryer and cook for 25-30 minutes.
5. Serve with low carb or gluten free bread and salad.

# White Bean Cheese Balls

Prep time: 15 minutes
Cooking time: 25 minutes

Ingredients:
- Two cups cooked white beans
- One cup chickpea flour
- One egg, beaten
- ¼ teaspoon black pepper
- ¼ teaspoon garlic powder
- Two cups mozzarella cheese

Directions:
1. Preheat your air fryer to 390 degrees F.
2. Combine all of the ingredients in a food processor and pulse (or stir by hand for a thicker consistency).
3. Use your hands to form balls.
4. Place in the air fryer and cook for 25 minutes.
5. Serve with a tomato sauce or salsa dip. Also delicious with homemade guacamole.

# Tomato and Cheese Black Bean Sticks

**Prep time: 15 minutes**
**Cooking time: 25 minutes**

## Ingredients:
- Two cups cooked black beans
- One cup chickpea flour
- One egg, beaten
- ¼ teaspoon black pepper
- ¼ teaspoon garlic powder
- Two cups mozzarella cheese
- One tomato, chopped

## Directions:
1. Preheat your air fryer to 390 degrees F.
2. Combine all of the ingredients in a food processor and pulse (or stir by hand for a thicker consistency).
3. Use your hands to form sticks.
4. Place in the air fryer and cook for 25 minutes.
5. Serve with guacamole.

# Veggie Filled Peppers

**Prep time: 15 minutes**
**Cooking time: 25 minutes**

## Ingredients:
- One cup shredded carrots (grated with a cheese grater)
- One cup shredded zucchini
- One cup shredded purple cabbage
- Two cups tomato sauce
- ¼ cup chopped onion
- ¼ teaspoon garlic powder
- ¼ teaspoon black pepper
- Two cups cream cheese
- Two cups grated havarti cheese
- 4 red bell peppers

## Directions:
1. Preheat your air fryer to 390 degrees F.
2. Combine the carrots, zucchini, purple cabbage, tomato sauce, onion, garlic, black pepper and cream cheese in a mixing bowl.
3. Cut the tops off of the bell peppers and remove the contents.
4. Spoon the carrot, zucchini and cabbage mixture into the peppers. Top with the havarti cheese.

5.   Place in the air fryer and cook for 25 minutes.

# Veggie Fingers
**Prep time: 15 minutes**
**Cooking time: 25 minutes**

## Ingredients:
- One cup shredded carrots (grated with a cheese grater)
- One cup grated celeriac (celery root)
- One cup shredded white cabbage
- One cup chopped fennel
- Two cups cream cheese
- One egg, beaten
- One cup grated cheddar cheese
- One teaspoon garlic powder
- Two cups chickpea flour

## Directions:
1. Preheat your air fryer to 390 degrees F.
2. Combine the carrots, celery root, cabbage, fennel, cream cheese, garlic and cheddar cheese.
3. Use your hands or a large mixing spoon to combine evenly. Use your hands to form "fingers".
4. Roll the veggie fingers in the egg. Then transfer to the chickpea flour and coat with the chickpea flour.
5. Place in the air fryer and cook for 25 minutes. Serve with a salsa dip or other tomato based dip of your choice.

# Lentil Cheese Balls
**Prep time: 15 minutes**
**Cooking time: 25 minutes**

## Ingredients:
- Two cups cooked red lentils
- Two cups cream cheese
- One cup swiss cheese
- One teaspoon garlic powder
- Two cups chickpea flour

## Directions:
1. Preheat your air fryer to 390 degrees F.
2. Combine the lentils, cream cheese, swiss cheese and garlic powder in a dish. Combine well using a large spoon or your hands.
3. Once the mixture is evenly distributed, use your hands to form balls.
4. Roll the balls in the chickpea flour.
5. Place in the air fryer and cook for 25 minutes. Serve with dip and salad.

# Fried Spinach Dip

**Prep time: 15 minutes**
**Cooking time: 25 minutes**

## Ingredients:
- Two cups sour cream
- One cup cream cheese
- One garlic clove, chopped
- Two cups havarti cheese, grated
- One cup frozen spinach, thawed and drained
- One tablespoon chickpea flour
- One teaspoon black pepper
- One teaspoon garlic powder

## Directions:
1. Preheat your air fryer to 390 degrees F.
2. Mix the sour cream, cream cheese, chopped garlic, spinach, chickpea flower, black pepper and garlic powder in a mixing bowl. Transfer to a heat safe dish.
3. Cover with the havarti cheese.
4. Cook in the air fryer for 25 minutes. Serve the dip with raw veggies, chips or use as a delicious sandwich condiment.

# Chickpea Burgers

**Prep time: 15 minutes**
**Cooking time: 25 minutes**

## Ingredients:
- Two cups cooked  chickpeas
- One cup grated zucchini
- One teaspoon garlic powder
- One cup cream cheese

## Directions:
1. Preheat your air fryer to 390 degrees F.
2. Place all of the ingredients in a food processor and pulse for a few seconds or stir by hand.
3. Use your hands to form burger patties.
4. Place in the air fryer and cook for 25-30 minutes.
5. Serve with low carb or gluten free bread and salad.

# Pistachio and Quinoa Burgers

**Prep time: 15 minutes**
**Cooking time: 25 minutes**
**Ingredients:**

- Two cups cooked quinoa
- One cup pistachios
- One teaspoon garlic powder
- One cup cream cheese
- One egg, beaten

### Directions:

1. Preheat your air fryer to 390 degrees F.
2. Place all of the ingredients in a food processor and pulse for a few seconds or stir by hand.
3. Use your hands to form burger patties.
4. Place in the air fryer and cook for 25-30 minutes.
5. Serve with low carb or gluten free bread and salad.

# Sweet Apple Walnut Balls

**Prep time: 15 minutes**
**Cooking time: 15 minutes**

**Ingredients:**

- Two cups grated apples
- One cup walnuts
- One cup dates
- One tablespoon butter (substitute with coconut oil for a vegan version)
- One teaspoon cinnamon

### Directions:

1. Preheat your air fryer to 390 degrees F.
2. Place all of the ingredients in a food processor and pulse for a few seconds or stir by hand.
3. Use your hands to form balls.
4. Place in the air fryer and cook for 15 minutes.
5. Serve as a snack, sweet appetizer or with ice cream as a dessert.

# Almond Plum Balls

**Prep time: 15 minutes**
**Cooking time: 15 minutes**

**Ingredients:**
- Two cups chopped plums
- One cup almonds
- One cup dates
- One tablespoon butter (substitute with coconut oil for a vegan version)
- One teaspoon cinnamon
- One pinch nutmeg

**Directions:**
1. Preheat your air fryer to 390 degrees F.
2. Place all of the ingredients in a food processor and pulse for a few seconds or stir by hand.
3. Use your hands to form balls.
4. Place in the air fryer and cook for 15 minutes.
5. Serve as a snack, sweet appetizer or with ice cream as a dessert.

# Sunflower Seed Broccoli Cheese Balls

**Prep time: 15 minutes**
**Cooking time: 15 minutes**

**Ingredients:**
- Two cups broccoli
- One cup sunflower seeds
- One cup mozzarella cheese (grated)
- One teaspoon garlic powder

**Directions:**
1. Preheat your air fryer to 390 degrees F.
2. Place all of the ingredients in a food processor and pulse for a few seconds or stir by hand.
3. Use your hands to form balls.
4. Place in the air fryer and cook for 15 minutes.

# Barbeque tofu

**Prep time: 5 minutes**
**Cooking time: 10 minutes**

## Ingredients:
- One package firm tofu with moisture squeezed out
- One cup barbeque sauce
- One tablespoon olive oil
- One tablespoon garlic powder
- One tablespoon black pepper
- One tablespoon honey

## Directions:
1. Preheat your Airfryer to 390 degrees F.
2. Combine all of the ingredients except the tofu in a mixing bowl.
3. Add the tofu and leave to marinade over night if possible.
4. Fry in the Airfryer for 10 minutes.

# Tofu egg rolls

**Prep time: 5 minutes**
**Cooking time: 10 minutes**

## Ingredients:
- 5 sheets of rice "paper" (egg roll sheets)
- two eggs, beaten
- One tablespoon onion powder
- One tablespoon garlic powder
- 1 ½ cups tofu cut into cube
- ½ cup cream cheese
- ½ cup shredded purple cabbage
- ½ cup pineapple
- ½ cup shredded carrots.

## Directions:
1. Preheat your Airfryer to 390 degrees F.
2. Mix the cheese, carrots, cabbage, tofu, pineapple and the onion and garlic powder.
3. Dip each rice "paper" in lukewarm water and remove quickly. Spread flat on a clean surface.
4. Distribute the tofu mix evenly among the rice sheets.
5. Wrap up and fold over the rice rolls.
6. Dip in the egg mix.
7. Place on a greased, heat safe form and cook in the Air fryer for 10 minutes.

# Avocado egg rolls

**Prep time: 5 minutes**
**Cooking time: 10 minutes**

## Ingredients:
- 5 sheets of rice "paper" (egg roll sheets)
- two eggs, beaten
- Three large avocados
- ½ cup herbed cream cheese
- One cup cubed mango

## Directions:
1. Preheat your Airfryer to 300 degrees F.
2. Mix the cheese, avocado and mango.
3. Dip each rice "paper" in lukewarm water and remove quickly. Spread flat on a clean surface.
4. Distribute the mango avocado mix evenly among the rice sheets.
5. Wrap up and fold over the rice rolls.
6. Dip in the egg mix.
7. Place on a greased, heat safe form and cook in the Air fryer for 10 minutes.

# Mango tofu

**Prep time: 5 minutes**
**Cooking time: 10 minutes**

## Ingredients:
- One package firm tofu with moisture squeezed out
- Two cups mango chunks, processed in a food processer to a puree
- One tablespoon honey

## Directions:
1. Preheat your Airfryer to 390 degrees F.
2. Combine all of the ingredients except the tofu in a mixing bowl.
3. Add the tofu and leave to marinade over night if possible.
4. Fry in the Airfryer for 10 minutes.

# Eggplant parmesan balls

**Prep time: 5 minutes**
**Cooking time: 15 minutes**

## Ingredients:
- One eggplant, cut into small pieces
- One tablespoon olive oil
- One tablespoon garlic powder
- One tablespoon black pepper
- One tablespoon honey
- Two tablespoons parmesan
- 2 eggs

## Directions:
1. Preheat your Airfryer to 390 degrees F.
2. Place all of the ingredients in a food processer and process until well combined.
3. Form balls with your hands.
4. Place in the Air fryer and cook for 15 minutes.

# Chickpea cheese bombs

**Prep time: 5 minutes**
**Cooking time: 15 minutes**

## Ingredients:
- Two cups chickpeas
- One tablespoon black pepper
- One tablespoon garlic powder
- ½ cup tomato sauce
- One egg, beaten
- Two cups swiss cheese

## Directions:
1. Preheat your Airfryer to 390 degrees F.
2. Place the ingredients in a food processor and pulse to combine.
3. Use your hands to form balls.
4. Roll the balls in additional cheese, if so desired.
5. Cook for 15 minutes.

# Fried cottage cheese

**Prep time: 5 minutes**
**Cooking time: 8 minutes**

**Ingredients:**

- 2 cups cottage cheese
- One egg, beaten
- One cup chickpea flour
- One tablespoon garlic powder

**Directions:**

1. Preheat your Airfryer to 390 degrees F.
2. Combine the garlic powder and chickpea flour.
3. Make the cottage cheese into several smaller balls using your hands to make them compact.
4. Dip them into the egg and then roll them in the chickpea flour.
5. Fry for 8 minutes.

# Fried spinach and cheese

**Prep time: 5 minutes**
**Cooking time: 10 minutes**

**Ingredients:**

- Two cups cream cheese
- One cup spinach, frozen and thawed
- One tablespoon garlic powder
- Two cups mozzarella
- One egg

**Directions:**

1. Preheat your Airfryer to 390 degrees F.
2. Combine all of the ingredients except the egg in a bowl.
3. Form balls using your hands.
4. Roll the balls (press down) to cover in mozzarella cheese.
5. Fry for 10 minutes.

# Veggie tacos

**Prep time: 5 minutes**
**Cooking time: 15 minutes**

## Ingredients:
- One package vegetarian ground beef (like the kind from quorn for example), thawed
- Four tablespoons taco seasoning (chili powder, paprika, garlic powder, onion powder, fenugreek)
- Two tablespoons water
- 6 soft tortilla or 6 crunchy tacos
- Your choice of taco fixings (sour cream, taco sauce, chopped tomato, lettuce, olives, etc)

## Directions:
1. Preheat your Airfryer to 390 degrees F.
2. Combine the veggie taco meat with the taco seasoning.
3. Place in the Airfryer.
4. Cook for 10 minutes.
5. Spoon into the tacos and warm for 5 additional minutes in the Airfryer.

# Cashew cheese and broccoli balls

**Prep time: 5 minutes**
**Cooking time: 10 minutes**

## Ingredients:
- Two cups cashew butter
- One cup broccoli florets, frozen and thawed
- One tablespoon garlic powder
- Two cups vegan cheese

## Directions:
1. Preheat your Airfryer to 390 degrees F.
2. Combine all of the ingredients in a bowl.
3. Form balls using your hands.
4. Fry for 10 minutes.

# Breaded stuffed peppers

**Prep time: 5 minutes**
**Cooking time: 15 minutes**

## Ingredients:

- Two green peppers, tops cut off with insides scooped out
- Two cups cream cheese
- One cup spinach, frozen and thawed
- One tablespoon garlic powder
- Two cups mozzarella
- One egg
- Three cups chickpea flour

## Directions:

1. Preheat your Airfryer to 390 degrees F.
2. Combine the cream cheese, mozzarella, spinach, garlic powder in a bowl.
3. Scoop the cream cheese mix into each pepper.
4. Dip the peppers in egg and then in chickpea flour.
5. Fry in the Airfryer for 15 minutes.

# Breaded black bean and sweet potatoes

**Prep time: 5 minutes**
**Cooking time: 15 minutes**

## Ingredients:

- Two sweet potatoes, peeled and cut into bite-sized pieces
- One cup cooked black beans
- One tablespoon garlic powder
- Two cups mozzarella
- One egg
- 2 cups chickpea flour

## Directions:

1. Preheat your Airfryer to 390 degrees F.
2. Process the sweet potatoes, black beans, garlic powder and mozzarella in a food processer.
3. Flatten the mixture into patties.
4. Dip first in the egg, and then in the chickpea flour.
5. Fry for 15 minutes in the Airfryer.

# Veggie stuffed sweet potatoes

**Prep time: 5 minutes**
**Cooking time: 18 minutes**

## Ingredients:
- Three large sweet potatoes, peeled
- One cup cooked quinoa
- ½ cup tofu pieces
- One cup peanut butter sauce (peanut butter, olive oil, garlic powder to make your own)

## Directions:
1. Preheat your Airfryer to 390 degrees F.
2. Place the sweet potatoes in the Air fryer and cook for 10 minutes.
3. Remove the sweet potatoes Scoop out some of the sweet potato and combine with the quinoa, tofu and peanut butter sauce.
4. Place back in the sweet potatoes.
5. Cook for another 8 minutes.

# Zucchini and cheese logs

**Prep time: 5 minutes**
**Cooking time: 10 minutes**

## Ingredients:
- Two zucchini, cut into halves lengthwise
- Two cups cream cheese
- ½ cup mozzarella
- One tablespoon garlic powder
- One tablespoon black pepper
- One pinch salt.

## Directions:
1. Preheat your Airfryer to 390 degrees F.
2. Mix the cream cheese with the mozzarella.
3. Place on top of the zucchini boats.
4. Sprinkle with garlic powder and pepper and a pinch of salt.
5. Cook in the Airfryer for 10 minutes.

# Falafel pockets

**Prep time: 5 minutes**
**Cooking time: 10 minutes**

## Ingredients:
- Two pita pockets
- Two cups pepper jack cheese
- 10 balls of falafel
- One cup hummus or baba ganoush

## Directions:
1. Preheat your Airfryer to 390 degrees F.
2. Place the other ingredients inside the pita pickets.
3. Brush with olive oil coconut oil and cook for 10 minutes.

# Stuffed veggie potatoes

**Prep time: 5 minutes**
**Cooking time: 25 minutes**

## Ingredients:
- 2 large potatoes
- 1 cup sour cream
- One tablespoon garlic powder
- One cup broccoli florets
- ½ cup finely chopped bell peppers
- One tomato, diced
- One cup cheddar cheese

## Directions:
1. Preheat your Airfryer to 390 degrees F.
2. Place the potatoes in the Air fryer. Poke holes in each potato using a fork. Cook for 15 minutes.
3. Mix the other ingredients in a bowl.
4. Remove the potatoes. And cut a slit down the middle of each one.
5. Remove some of the potato flesh from inside the potato.
6. Mix with the sour cream combo.
7. Place all of the mixture ingredients in each potato. They will be overflowing, so place on a dish or optionally wrap with tin foil.
8. Cook for 10 more minutes.

# Lemon Cashew Seitan

**Prep time: 5 minutes**
**Cooking time: 15 minutes**

## Ingredients:

- 3 cups seitan, cut into bite-sized pieces
- Two cups cashew butter
- ½ cup cashew pieces
- Two tablespoons lemon juice
- One tablespoon black pepper

## Directions:

1. Preheat your Airfryer to 390 degrees F.
2. Combine the cashew butter, cashews, black pepper and lemon juice.
3. Then add the seitan.
4. Cook in the Airfryer for 15 minutes.

# Tomato Tempeh

**Prep time: 5 minutes**
**Cooking time: 15 minutes**

## Ingredients:

- One package tempeh, cut into strips
- Two cups tomato sauce
- One teaspoon crushed red pepper
- One tablespoon back pepper

## Directions:

1. Preheat your Airfryer to 390 degrees F.
2. Combine the sauce, crushed red pepper and black pepper. Add the tempeh.
3. Place in the Air fryer and cook for 15 minutes.

# Mushroom Tempeh

**Prep time: 5 minutes**
**Cooking time: 15 minutes**

## Ingredients:
- One package seitan, cut into strips
- One tablespoon garlic powder
- One tablespoon black pepper
- One cup mushrooms
- One cup coconut milk

## Directions:
1. Preheat your Airfryer to 390 degrees F.
2. Place all the ingredients together in a pan and cook for 15 minutes in your Airfryer.

# Vegetarian Spicy "Chicken"

**Prep time: 5 minutes**
**Cooking time: 15 minutes**

## Ingredients:
- 3 quorn "chicken " filets
- One inch worth root of ginger, chopped finely
- Two cloves garlic, finely chopped
- One tablespoon olive oil
- One tablespoon crushed red pepper
- One cup tomato sauce

## Directions:
1. Preheat your Airfryer to 390 degrees F.
2. Mix the tomato sauce with the ginger, garlic, olive oil, crushed red pepper.
3. Pour into heat safe dish.
4. Add the quorn "chicken".
5. Cook for 15 minutes.

# Dessert

## Chocolate cupcakes

**Prep time: 10 minutes**
**Cooking time: 15 minutes**

**Ingredients**:

- 4 tablespoons cocoa powder
- 1 cup flour
- 1 teaspoon baking powder
- 2 eggs
- 1 cup sugar
- 0.5 cup coconut oil, melted to liquid form
- 0.5 cup whole milk
- 1 teaspoon vanilla extract

**Directions:**

1. Preheat the Airfryer to 360 degrees F.
2. Combine the dry ingredients in one mixing bowl (flour, sugar, cocoa powder, baking powder).
3. Combine the wet ingredients in another mixing bowl (eggs, coconut oil, milk, vanilla extract). Beat the eggs and blend ingredients well.
4. Transfer the wet mixture into the dry mixture. Mix with a hand mixer or whisk by hand.
5. Place cupcake cups in the Airfryer and pour the batter in carefully.
6. Bake for 15 minutes.
7. Top with chocolate frosting, coconut cream or whipped cream for an easy and sweet treat.

# Cherry chocolate cupcakes

**Prep time: 10 minutes**
**Cooking time: 15 minutes**

Ingredients:

- 4 tablespoons cocoa powder
- 1 cup flour
- 1 teaspoon baking powder
- 2 eggs
- 1 cup sugar
- 0.5 cup coconut oil, melted to liquid form
- 0.5 cup whole milk
- 1 teaspoon vanilla extract
- 1/2 cup frozen (thawed) or fresh cherries

Directions:

1. Preheat the Airfryer to 360 degrees F.
2. Combine the dry ingredients in one mixing bowl (flour, sugar, cocoa powder, baking powder).
3. Combine the wet ingredients in another mixing bowl (eggs, coconut oil, milk, vanilla extract). Beat the eggs and blend ingredients well.
4. Transfer the wet mixture into the dry mixture. Mix with a hand mixer or whisk by hand. Fold in the cherries carefully with a spatula.
5. Place cupcake cups in the Airfryer and pour the batter in carefully. Bake for 15 minutes.
6. Top with chocolate frosting, coconut cream or whipped cream for an easy and sweet treat. Garnish with one fresh cherry.

# Coconut cookies

**Prep time: 10 minutes**
**Cooking time: 12 minutes**

Ingredients:
- 1 cup flour
- 2 eggs
- 1/2 cup melted coconut oil
- 1 cup sugar or coconut sugar
- 1 cup shredded coconut
- 2 tablespoons coconut milk
- 1 teaspoon vanilla extract
- 1/2 teaspoon baking powder

Directions:
1. Preheat the Airfryer to 360 degrees F.
2. In a bowl, combine the flour, coconut and baking powder and sugar.
3. Combine the remaining ingredients (eggs, coconut milk, vanilla extract) in a separate bowl and whisk to beat the eggs.
4. Pour the wet ingredients into the bowl with the dry ingredients. Combine with a hand mixer or whisk.
5. Form balls with the dough with your hands. Place the cookie balls into an oven safe form and place that in the Airfryer. (You will need to make 2-3 batches to use up all the dough.)
6. Bake for 12-15 minutes.
7. Top the cookies with a little more shredded coconut.

# Apple crisp
**Prep time: 10 minutes**
**Cooking time: 10 minutes**

**Ingredients:**
- 4 apples
- 1/2 cup lightly cooked oats
- 4 tablespoons maple syrup
- 2 teaspoons cinnamon
- 1 teaspoon sugar

**Directions:**
1. Preheat the Airfryer to 360 degrees F.
2. Peel, core and slice the apples into thin slices. Then add the maple syrup, cinnamon and oats. Mix well by hand.
3. Place the mixture in an oven safe form.
4. Sprinkle with sugar and an additional pinch of cinnamon.
5. Bake for 10 minutes.
6. Serve with vanilla ice cream and/or whipped cream.

# Blueberry crisp

**Prep time: 10 minutes**
**Cooking time: 10 minutes**

**Ingredients**:
- 2 cups blueberries (fresh or frozen)
- 3 tablespoons maple syrup (or honey)
- 1 tablespoon cinnamon
- 1 teaspoon sugar
- 1/4 cup lightly cooked oats
- 1 teaspoon vanilla extract

**Directions:**
1. Preheat the Airfryer to 360 degrees F.
2. Combine all of the ingredients in a mixing bowl. Stir by hand.
3. Transfer the ingredients into an oven safe form.
4. Cook for 10 minutes. Enjoy with vanilla ice cream!

# Peach pie

**Prep time: 10 minutes**
**Cooking time: 15 minutes**

**Ingredients**:
- 2 cups sliced peaches
- 3 tablespoons of maple syrup
- 1 tablespoon sugar
- 1 teaspoon vanilla extract
- 1 tablespoon liquefied coconut oil
- 1 pie crust

**Directions:**
1. Preheat the Airfryer to 360 degrees F.
2. Combine the peaches, syrup, sugar, vanilla in a bowl and mix by hand.
3. Put the pie crust into an oven safe form that fits in the Airfryer. Brush with the coconut oil.
4. Put the peach mixture into the pie crust. Fold over any edges that hang out over the form.
5. Bake for 15 minutes. Serve with ice cream or whipped cream. A garnish of mint adds a gourmet touch.

# Plum crisp

**Prep time: 10 minutes**
**Cooking time: 10 minutes**

Ingredients:
- 2 cups sliced plums
- 3 tablespoons of honey or maple syrup
- 1/2 cup lightly cooked oats
- 1 teaspoon vanilla extract
- 1 tablespoon sugar
- 1 teaspoon cinnamon

Directions:
1. Preheat the Airfryer to 360 degrees F.
2. Put all of the ingredients in a bowl and mix by hand.
3. Transfer the ingredients to an oven safe form. Place in the Airfryer and bake for 10 minutes.
4. Serve with vanilla or chocolate ice cream.

# Nectarine bowl

**Prep time: 10 minutes**
**Cooking time: 12 minutes**

Ingredients:
- 2 cups sliced nectarines with skin still on
- 3 tablespoons maple syrup
- 1 tablespoon sugar
- 1/2 cup whipped cream
- 1 frozen, pre-made pie crust of your choice
- 1 tablespoon coconut oil or butter

Directions:
1. Preheat the Airfryer to 360 degrees F.
2. Combine the nectarines with the syrup, sugar and whipped cream in a bowl and set aside.
3. Put the pie crust into the oven safe form that fits your Airfryer. Brush with oil or butter.
4. Bake the crust until golden brown (about 12 minutes).
5. Remove the crust and allow cooling for a few minutes. Then spoon in the nectarine cream mixture and enjoy!

# Strawberry shortcake

**Prep time: 10 minutes**
**Cooking time: 15 minutes**

**Ingredients:**
- 2 cups strawberries
- 1 cup whipped cream
- 1 cup flour
- 1 teaspoon baking soda
- 1 pinch salt
- 2 eggs
- 1/4 milk
- 2 tablespoons melted butter or coconut oil

**Directions:**
1. Preheat the Airfryer to 360 degrees F.
2. Combine the flour, baking soda, salt in one bowl.
3. In another bowl beat the eggs, add in the milk and the coconut oil or butter and stir.
4. Then combine the wet ingredients with the dry ingredients in one bowl. Mix by hand or using an electric mixer.
5. Form shortbread cakes and place on an oven safe form. Brush with a bit more coconut oil or butter.
6. Bake in the Airfryer for 12 minutes. Check progress and bake for 3 more minutes if necessary.
7. Top with whipped cream and strawberries and garnish with a sprig of mint for a perfect summertime treat.

# Carrot cake cupcakes

**Prep time: 10 minutes**
**Cooking time: 12 minutes**

**Ingredients**:
- 1 cup flour
- 1 teaspoon baking powder
- 1/2 cup sugar
- 2 teaspoons cinnamon
- 1/2 cup grated carrots
- 1/2 teaspoon nutmeg
- 2 eggs
- 1/2 cup milk
- 3 tablespoons coconut oil or butter, liquefied

**Directions:**
1. Preheat Airfryer to 360 degrees F.
2. Combine the flour, baking powder, sugar, cinnamon and nutmeg in one bowl.
3. Mix the wet ingredients in another (eggs, milk, butter).
4. Transfer the contents of the wet ingredient bowl into the dry ingredient bowl. Mix with a hand mixer. Then fold in the shredded carrots.
5. Carefully place cupcake cups into the Airfryer and carefully pour in batter.
6. Bake for 12-15 minutes.
7. Top with whipped cream or vanilla frosting.

# Molten Lava Cakes

**Prep time: 20 minutes**
**Cooking time: 10 minutes**

## Ingredients:

- 1.5 tbsp self-rising flour
- 3.5 tbsp pure cane sugar (baker's sugar)
- 3.5 oz butter
- 3.5 oz chopped dark chocolate
- 2 eggs

## Directions:

1. Preheat your air fryer to 375 degrees F.
2. Lightly grease and flour 4 standard sized oven safe ramekins.
3. Melt chocolate and butter in one bowl. You could do it in your microwave.
4. Whisk eggs by hand mixer for a few minutes and then add in sugar. Continue beating until frothy.
5. Add flour to your chocolate mixture. Don't forget previously to sift the flour.
6. Pour chocolate and flour mixture into eggs. Stir until smooth.
7. Spoon batter into prepared ramekins (about ¾ full).
8. Bake in air fryer for 10 minutes.
9. Let cool in ramekins for 2 minutes.

# Fried Cinnamon Bananas

**Prep time: 15 minutes**
**Cooking time: 7 minutes**

## Ingredients:

- 3 tbsp coconut oil
- 8 bananas
- 2 eggs
- 1/2 cup corn flour
- 3 tbsp cinnamon sugar
- 1 cup bread crumbs

## Directions:

1. Preheat your air fryer to 280 degrees F.
2. Heat coconut oil in pan and add breadcrumbs. Stir for 4-5 minutes. Remove from burner and pour in a bowl.
3. Halve bananas. Don't forget to peel them previously.
4. Roll each banana piece first in flour, then in eggs and finally in bread crumbs with oil.
5. Place bananas in air fryer basket.
6. Powder with sugar.
7. Bake in airfryer for 7 minutes.

# Apple Chips

**Prep time: 10 minutes**
**Cooking time: 15 minutes**

## Ingredients:
- 1 apple, peeled, cored and thinly sliced horizontally
- 1/2 tsp ground cinnamon
- 1 tbsp sugar
- salt

## Directions:
1. Preheat your air fryer to 390 degrees F.
2. Peele, core and slice apple thinly.
3. Put apple slices on a baking sheet.
4. In a bowl, combine cinnamon, sugar and pinch of salt.
5. Sprinkle the mixture over the slices.
6. Put it into airfryer basket.
7. Bake in airfryer for 15 minutes.

# Chocolate Cake

**Prep time: 15 minutes**
**Cooking time: 15 minutes**

## Ingredients:
- 1.75 oz caster sugar
- 1.75 oz butter
- 1 egg
- 1 tbsp apricot jam
- 1.75 oz plain flour
- 1 tbsp cocoa
- pinch of salt

## Directions:
1. Preheat your air fryer to 320 degrees F.
2. Lightly grease a small ring cake tin.
3. In a bowl beat butter (previously melted) with caster sugar until it becomes creamy.
4. Add in 1 egg and apricot jam. Mix it.
5. In another bowl, sift flour, salt & cocoa. Stir it.
6. Pour the mixture into the bowl with butter. Stir until smooth.
7. Spoon the batter to the tin.
8. Bake for 13-15 minutes.

# Apple Dumplings
**Prep time: 15 minutes**
**Cooking time: 25 minutes**

## Ingredients:
- 4 small apples
- 4 tbsp sultanas
- 2 tbsp brown sugar
- 4 sheets puff pastry
- 2 tbsp butter

## Directions:
1. Preheat your air fryer to 350 degrees F.
2. Wash, peel and core the apples.
3. Mix brown sugar and raisins.
4. Stuff the apple with the raisins mixture.
5. Put each apple in the center of puff pastry sheet.
6. Fold the pastry around the apple.
7. Place apple dumplings on a foil in order to avoid falling of juice into air fryer.
8. Melt the butter.
9. Brush the dough with the butter.
10. Put apple dumplings in air fryer basket.
11. Cook for 20-25 minutes.

# Red wine chocolate cake cup
**Prep time: 5 minutes**
**Cooking time: 15 minutes**

## Ingredients:
- ¼ cup red wine
- One tablespoon honey
- ½ cup coconut sugar or brown sugar
- One cup all purpose flour
- ½ cup butter
- ¼ cup baking cocoa
- One egg
- One teaspoon baking powder

## Directions:
1. Preheat your Airfryer to 390 degrees F.
2. Mix together all of the ingredients.
3. Place in a greased heat safe small dish.
4. Cook for 15 minutes.

# Blueberry cream cheese cake

**Prep time: 5 minutes**
**Cooking time: 15 minutes**

**Ingredients:**
- One cup blueberry jam
- Two  cups cream cheese
- One tablespoon honey
- ½ cup coconut sugar or brown sugar
- One cup all purpose flour
- ½ cup butter
- 2 eggs

**Directions:**
1. Preheat your Airfryer to 390 degrees F.
2. Mix together all of the ingredients.
3. Place in a greased heat safe dish.
4. Cook for 15 minutes.

# Vanilla cream

**Prep time: 5 minutes**
**Cooking time: 15 minutes**

**Ingredients:**
- 2 cups cream cheese
- 2 tablespoons honey
- ½ cup full fat cream
- ½ cup brown sugar
- One egg
- One tablespoon vanilla extract

**Directions:**
1. Preheat your Airfryer to 390 degrees F.
2. Mix together all of the ingredients.
3. Place in a greased heat safe dish.
4. Cook for 15 minutes.

# Strawberry pocket

**Prep time: 5 minutes**
**Cooking time: 18 minutes**

## Ingredients:
- Flaky pastry dough
- One tablespoon butter
- Two cups frozen and thawed strawberries
- One tablespoon honey
- One tablespoon brown sugar

## Directions:
1. Preheat your Airfryer to 390 degrees F.
2. Mix together the strawberries, honey and sugar.
3. Brush the pastry dough with butter.
4. Place the strawberries on the dough and fold over.
5. Place in a greased heat safe small dish.
6. Cook for 18 minutes.

# Chocolate Strudel

**Prep time: 5 minutes**
**Cooking time: 18 minutes**

## Ingredients:
- Flaky pastry dough
- One tablespoon butter
- Two cups chocolate pudding (homemade or your choice of chocolate pudding)

## Directions:
1. Preheat your Airfryer to 390 degrees F.
2. Brush the pastry dough with butter.
3. Spoon an even amount of pudding on each part of the dough, leaving one side bare.
4. Fold over the side without the pudding. Pinch the edges.
5. Place in a greased heat safe small dish.
7. Cook in the Airfryer for 18 minutes.

# Apple cake

**Prep time: 5 minutes**
**Cooking time: 15 minutes**

**Ingredients:**
- Two cups apple sauce
- One tablespoon cinnamon
- One tablespoon baking powder
- One tablespoon honey
- ½ cup coconut sugar or brown sugar
- One cup all purpose flour
- ½ cup butter
- 2 eggs

**Directions:**
1. Preheat your Airfryer to 390 degrees F.
2. Mix together all of the ingredients.
3. Place in a greased heat safe dish.
4. Cook for 15 minutes.

# Quick crunchy apple crisp

**Prep time: 5 minutes**
**Cooking time: 15 minutes**

**Ingredients:**
- 8 apples, peeled and sliced
- One cup brown sugar
- One cup steel cut, rolled oats
- ½ cup chopped walnuts
- One tablespoon honey
- One cup butter

**Directions:**
1. Preheat your Airfryer to 390 degrees F.
2. Mix together all of the ingredients.
3. Place in a greased heat safe dish.
4. Cook for 15 minutes.
5. Serve with vanilla ice cream or whipped cream.

# Walnuts and pears crisp

**Prep time: 5 minutes**
**Cooking time: 15 minutes**

**Ingredients:**
- 8 pears, peeled and sliced
- One cup brown sugar
- One cup almond flour
- One  cup chopped walnuts
- One tablespoon honey
- One cup butter

**Directions:**
1. Preheat your Airfryer to 390 degrees F.
2. Mix together all of the ingredients.
3. Place in a greased heat safe dish.
4. Cook for 15 minutes. Serve with vanilla ice cream or whipped cream.

# Marzipan liquorice cake

**Prep time: 5 minutes**
**Cooking time: 18 minutes**

**Ingredients:**
- One cup almond flour
- cup almond butter
- One cup liquorice powder
- 2 eggs
- One cup cream cheese
- One teaspoon almond essence
- One cup sugar
- One cup butter
- One teaspoon baking powder

**Directions:**
1. Preheat your Airfryer to 390 degrees F.
2. Mix together all of the ingredients.
3. Place in a greased heat safe dish.
4. Cook for 18 minutes.
5. Serve with vanilla ice cream or whipped cream.

# Pumpkin cheesecake

**Prep time: 5 minutes**
**Cooking time: 15 minutes**

**Ingredients:**
- Two cups cream cheese
- Two cups pumpkin pie mix (including sugar, cloves, cinnamon)
- Two eggs

**Directions:**
1. Preheat your Airfryer to 390 degrees F.
2. Mix together all of the ingredients.
3. Place in a greased heat safe dish.
4. Cook for 15 minutes. Serve with vanilla ice cream or whipped cream.

# Blueberry Protein Cake

**Prep time: 5 minutes**
**Cooking time: 15 minutes**

**Ingredients:**
- One cup frozen and thawed wild blueberries
- 3 cups almond flour
- One cup butter
- One cup apple sauce
- 2 eggs
- One cup cream cheese

**Directions:**
1. Preheat your Airfryer to 390 degrees F.
2. Mix together all of the ingredients.
3. Place in a greased heat safe dish.
4. Cook for 15 minutes.
5. Serve with vanilla ice cream or whipped cream

# Coconut Cream Cheese Puffs

**Prep time: 5 minutes**
**Cooking time: 15 minutes**

## Ingredients:
- 2 cups cream cheese
- 2 eggs
- 3 tablespoons honey
- One cup coconut

## Directions:
1. Preheat your Airfryer to 390 degrees F.
2. Mix together all of the ingredients.
3. Use your hands to form balls.
4. Place in a greased heat safe dish.
5. Cook for 12 minutes.

# Raspberry Tart

**Prep time: 5 minutes**
**Cooking time: 18 minutes**

## Ingredients:
- Flaky pastry dough
- One tablespoon butter
- Two cups raspberry jam
- Two tablespoons powdered sugar

## Directions:
1. Preheat your Airfryer to 390 degrees F.
2. Brush the pastry dough with butter.
3. Spoon an even amount of jam on each part of the dough, leaving one side bare.
4. Fold over the side without the jam. Pinch the edges.
5. Place in a greased heat safe small dish.
6. Cook in the Airfryer for 18 minutes. Dust with the powdered sugar.

# Cherry chocolate beet cake

**Prep time: 5 minutes**
**Cooking time: 15 minutes**

## Ingredients:
- One cup cherry jam
- One tablespoon beet juice
- One teaspoon vanilla extract
- One tablespoon honey
- ½ cup coconut sugar or brown sugar
- One cup all purpose flour
- ½ cup butter
- ¼ cup baking cocoa
- One egg
- One teaspoon baking powder

## Directions:
1. Preheat your Airfryer to 390 degrees F.
2. Mix together all of the ingredients.
3. Place in a greased heat safe small dish.
4. Cook for 15 minutes.

# Chocolate Peanut Butter Cake

**Prep time: 5 minutes**
**Cooking time: 15 minutes**

## Ingredients:
- One bar dark chocolate cut up into pieces
- One cup peanut butter, softened by warming
- One tablespoon butter, softened and combined with the peanut butter
- 1 cup coconut sugar or brown sugar
- One cup all purpose flour
- ½ cup butter
- ¼ cup baking cocoa
- One egg
- One teaspoon baking powder

## Directions:
1. Preheat your Airfryer to 390 degrees F.
2. Mix together all of the ingredients.
3. Place in a greased heat safe small dish.
4. Cook for 15 minutes.

# Chocolate Coffee Cake

**Prep time: 5 minutes**
**Cooking time: 15 minutes**

**Ingredients:**
- One cup coffee
- One tablespoon honey
- One cup white sugar
- One cup all purpose flour
- ½ cup butter
- ¼ cup baking cocoa
- One egg
- One teaspoon baking powder
- One cup brown sugar

**Directions:**
1. Preheat your Airfryer to 390 degrees F.
2. Mix together all of the ingredients. Reserve half of the brown sugar.
3. Place in a greased heat safe small dish.
4. Cook for 18 minutes. Remove from the Airfryer and dust with brown sugar.

# Swirl Cheesecake

**Prep time: 5 minutes**
**Cooking time: 18 minutes**

**Ingredients:**
- 3 cups cream cheese
- 3 eggs
- One teaspoon vanilla extract
- One cup full fat cream
- One cup sugar
- One tablespoon honey
- One cup raspberry jam

**Directions:**
1. Preheat your Airfryer to 390 degrees F.
2. Mix together all of the ingredients except the raspberry jam.
3. Add a little of the jam at a time. Use a fork to swirl it through the cheese mixture.
4. Place in a greased heat safe small dish.
5. Cook for 18 minutes.

# Pumpkin Pudding
**Prep time: 5 minutes**
**Cooking time: 15 minutes**

**Ingredients:**
- Three cups pumpkin puree
- Three tablespoons honey
- One tablespoon ginger
- One tablespoon cinnamon
- One teaspoon clove
- One teaspoon nutmeg
- One cup full fat cream
- Two eggs
- One cup brown sugar

**Directions:**
1. Preheat your Airfryer to 390 degrees F.
2. Mix together all of the ingredients.
3. Place in a greased heat safe small dish.
4. Cook for 15 minutes. Serve topped with whipped cream.

# Honey Oatmeal Almond Cake
**Prep time: 5 minutes**
**Cooking time: 18 minutes**

**Ingredients:**
- Three tablespoons honey
- One cup oatmeal
- Two cups almond flour
- 2 eggs
- One teaspoon baking powder
- One cup brown sugar
- ⅓ cup whipping cream
- One cup butter

**Directions:**
1. Preheat your Airfryer to 390 degrees F.
2. Mix together all of the ingredients.
3. Place in a greased heat safe small dish.
4. Cook for 18 minutes.

# Banana Cream Chocolate Cake
**Prep time: 5 minutes**
**Cooking time: 16 minutes**

## Ingredients:
- One cup cream cheese
- 3 tablespoons honey
- 2 ripe bananas, mashed
- One cup full fat cream
- One tablespoon cocoa
- 2 eggs, beaten
- One cup sugar

## Directions:
1. Preheat your Airfryer to 390 degrees F.
2. Mix together all of the ingredients.
3. Place in a greased heat safe small dish.
4. Cook for 18 minutes.

# Calorie Tables

## Vegetables

| 3 oz of food | Calories | Fat | Protein | Carbs | Fibe |
|---|---|---|---|---|---|
| Pecans | 691 | 72 | 9g | 14g | 10g |
| Walnuts | 654 | 65 | 15g | 14g | 7g |
| Hazelnuts | 628 | 61 | 15g | 17g | 10g |
| Sunflower Seeds | 584 | 51 | 21g | 20g | 9g |
| Almonds | 575 | 49 | 21g | 22g | 12g |
| Sesame Seeds | 573 | 50 | 18g | 23g | 12g |
| Pumpkin Seeds | 541 | 46 | 25g | 18g | 4g |
| Soybeans | 446 | 20 | 36g | 30g | 9g |
| Quinoa | 368 | 6g | 14g | 64g | 7g |
| Beans, Pinto | 347 | 1g | 21g | 63g | 15g |
| Black Beans | 341 | 1g | 22g | 62g | 15g |
| Beans, Kidney | 337 | 1g | 23g | 61g | 15g |
| Beans, Navy | 337 | 1g | 22g | 61g | 24g |
| Cranberry Beans | 335 | 1g | 23g | 60g | 25g |
| Mushrooms, Shiitake | 296 | 1g | 10g | 75g | 11g |
| Avocado | 160 | 15 | 2g | 9g | 7g |
| Garlic | 149 | 0g | 6g | 33g | 2g |
| Yams | 118 | 0g | 2g | 28g | 4g |
| Bananas | 89 | 0g | 1g | 23g | 3g |
| Corn | 86 | 1g | 3g | 19g | 3g |
| Sweet Potato | 86 | 0g | 2g | 20g | 3g |
| Pomegranates | 83 | 1g | 2g | 19g | 4g |
| Peas | 81 | 0g | 5g | 14g | 5g |
| Potatoes, Russet | 79 | 0g | 2g | 18g | 1g |
| Parsnips | 75 | 0g | 1g | 18g | 5g |
| Figs | 74 | 0g | 1g | 19g | 3g |
| Shallots | 72 | 0g | 3g | 17g | 0g |
| Kumquats | 71 | 1g | 2g | 16g | 6g |

| | | | | | |
|---|---|---|---|---|---|
| Potatoes, Red | 70 | 0g | 2g | 16g | 2g |
| Guava | 68 | 1g | 3g | 14g | 5g |
| Grapes | 67 | 0g | 1g | 17g | 1g |
| Cherries | 63 | 0g | 1g | 16g | 2g |
| Leeks | 61 | 0g | 1g | 14g | 2g |
| Pears | 58 | 0g | 0g | 15g | 3g |
| Blueberries | 57 | 0g | 1g | 14g | 2g |
| Tangerines | 53 | 0g | 1g | 13g | 2g |
| Apples | 52 | 0g | 0g | 14g | 2g |
| Raspberries | 52 | 1g | 1g | 12g | 6g |
| Kale | 50 | 1g | 3g | 10g | 2g |
| Pineapple | 50 | 0g | 1g | 13g | 1g |
| Apricots | 48 | 0g | 1g | 11g | 2g |
| Artichokes | 47 | 0g | 3g | 11g | 5g |
| Oranges | 47 | 0g | 1g | 12g | 2g |
| Cranberries | 46 | 0g | 0g | 12g | 5g |
| Beets | 43 | 0g | 2g | 10g | 3g |
| Blackberries | 43 | 0g | 1g | 10g | 5g |
| Celeriac | 42 | 0g | 1g | 9g | 2g |
| Grapefruit | 42 | 0g | 1g | 11g | 2g |
| Sugar Snap Peas | 42 | 0g | 3g | 8g | 3g |
| Carrots | 41 | 0g | 1g | 10g | 3g |
| Acorn Squash | 40 | 0g | 1g | 10g | 1g |
| Onion | 40 | 0g | 1g | 9g | 2g |
| Papaya | 39 | 0g | 1g | 10g | 2g |
| Peaches | 39 | 0g | 1g | 10g | 1g |
| Mushrooms | 37 | 0g | 2g | 7g | 3g |
| Honeydew | 36 | 0g | 1g | 9g | 1g |
| Rutabagas | 36 | 0g | 1g | 8g | 3g |
| Broccoli | 34 | 0g | 3g | 7g | 3g |
| Cantaloupe | 34 | 0g | 1g | 9g | 1g |
| Serrano Pepper | 32 | 0g | 2g | 8g | 4g |
| Strawberries | 32 | 0g | 1g | 8g | 2g |
| Green Beans | 31 | 0g | 2g | 7g | 3g |
| Okra | 31 | 0g | 2g | 7g | 3g |
| Spaghetti Squash | 31 | 1g | 1g | 7g | 0g |
| Sweet Red Peppers | 31 | 0g | 1g | 6g | 2g |
| Collards | 30 | 0g | 2g | 6g | 4g |
| Limes | 30 | 0g | 1g | 11g | 3g |
| Watermelon | 30 | 0g | 1g | 8g | 0g |
| Lemons | 29 | 0g | 1g | 9g | 3g |
| Turnips | 28 | 0g | 1g | 6g | 2g |
| Banana Peppers | 27 | 0g | 2g | 5g | 3g |
| Sweet Yellow | 27 | 0g | 1g | 6g | 1g |

| Peppers | | | | | |
|---|---|---|---|---|---|
| Mustard Greens | 26 | 0g | 3g | 5g | 3g |
| Cabbage | 25 | 0g | 1g | 6g | 3g |
| Cauliflower | 25 | 0g | 2g | 5g | 3g |
| Eggplant | 24 | 0g | 1g | 6g | g |
| Spinach | 23 | 0g | 3g | 4g | 2g |
| Rhubarb | 21 | 0g | 1g | 5g | 2g |
| Asparagus | 20 | 0g | 2g | 4g | 2g |
| Sweet Green Pepper | 20 | 0g | 1g | 5g | 2g |
| Swiss Chard | 19 | 0g | 2g | 4g | 2g |
| Tomatoes | 18 | 0g | 1g | 4g | 1g |
| Celery | 16 | 0g | 1g | 3g | 2g |
| Radish | 16 | 0g | 1g | 3g | 2g |
| Summer Squash | 16 | 0g | 1g | 3g | 1g |
| Cucumbers | 15 | 0g | 1g | 4g | 0g |
| Lettuce | 15 | 0g | 1g | 3g | 1g |

# Meat and Poultry

| 3 oz of cooked food | Calories | Fat | Protein |
|---|---|---|---|
| *Chicken (with skin)* | | | |
| Wing, roasted | 240 | 16g | 23g |
| Thigh, roasted | 210 | 13g | 21g |
| Whole, without neck and giblets, roasted | 200 | 11g | 23g |
| Drumstick, roasted | 180 | 9g | 23g |
| Breast, roasted | 170 | 7g | 25g |
| Turkey (with skin) | | | |
| Wing, roasted | 190 | 10g | 23g |
| Thigh, roasted | 190 | 10g | 23g |
| Drumstick, roasted | 170 | 8g | 23g |
| Whole, without neck and giblets, roasted | 170 | 8g | 24g |
| Breast, roasted | 160 | 6g | 24g |
| *Beef (with fat trimmed to 1/8 inch)* | | | |
| Rib, roast, large end, roasted | 300 | 24g | 19g |
| Brisket, point half, braised | 300 | 23g | 21g |
| Chuck, blade roast, braised | 290 | 21g | 22g |
| Brisket, whole, braised | 280 | 21g | 22g |
| Brisket, flat half, braised | 250 | 16g | 25g |
| Chuck, arm pot roast, braised | 250 | 16g | 25g |
| Rib, steak, small end, broiled | 240 | 17g | 22g |
| Loin, top loin steak, broiled | 220 | 14g | 22g |
| Loin, tenderloin steak, broiled | 220 | 14g | 22g |
| Round, bottom round steak, braised | 210 | 10g | 28g |
| Loin, sirloin steak, broiled | 200 | 12g | 23g |
| Round, tip roast, roasted | 180 | 10g | 23g |
| Round, eye round steak, roasted | 170 | 8g | 24g |
| Round, top round steak, broiled | 170 | 8g | 26g |
| *Pork* | | | |
| Spareribs, braised | 330 | 25g | 24g |
| Loin, country style ribs, roasted | 280 | 21g | 20g |

| | | | |
|---|---|---|---|
| Shoulder, blade steak, broiled | 220 | 15g | 21g |
| Loin, sirloin roast, roasted | 190 | 11g | 22g |
| Loin, rib chop, broiled | 190 | 11g | 21g |
| Loin, chop, broiled | 180 | 9g | 22g |
| Loin, top loin chop, boneless, broiled | 160 | 8g | 22g |
| Loin, top roast, boneless, roasted | 160 | 7g | 22g |
| Loin tenderloin, roasted | 120 | 3.5g | 22g |
| *Lamb (with fat trimmed to 1/8 inch)* | | | |
| Rib roast, roasted | 290 | 23g | 18g |
| Shoulder, blade chop, broiled | 280 | 20g | 24g |
| Shoulder, arm chop, broiled | 280 | 19g | 26g |
| Loin chop, broiled | 250 | 17g | 22g |
| Leg, sirloin half, roasted | 240 | 17g | 21g |
| Leg, whole, roasted | 200 | 12g | 22g |
| Shank, roasted | 180 | 10g | 22g |
| Leg, shank half, roasted | 180 | 10g | 23g |

# Fish & Seafood

| 3 oz of cooked food | Calories | Fat | Protein | Carbs |
|---|---|---|---|---|
| Blue Carb | 100 | 1g | 20g | 0g |
| Catfish | 130 | 6g | 17g | 0g |
| Clams | 110 | 1.5g | 17g | 6g |
| Cod | 90 | 1g | 20g | 0g |
| Flounder/Sole | 100 | 1.5g | 19g | 0g |
| Haddock | 100 | 1g | 21g | 0g |
| Halibut | 120 | 2g | 23g | 0g |
| Lobster | 80 | 0.5g | 17g | 1g |
| Ocean Perch | 110 | 2g | 21g | 0g |
| Orange Roughy | 80 | 1g | 16g | 0g |
| Oysters, 12 medium | 100 | 4g | 10g | 6g |
| Pollock | 90 | 1g | 20g | 0g |
| Rainbow Trout | 140 | 6g | 20g | 0g |
| Rockfish | 110 | 2g | 21g | 0g |
| Salmon | 200 | 10g | 24g | 0g |
| Scallops, 6 large | 140 | 1g | 27g | 5g |
| Shrimp | 100 | 1.5g | 21g | 0g |
| Swordfish | 120 | 6g | 16g | 0g |
| Tilapia | 110 | 2.5g | 22g | 0g |
| Tuna | 130 | 1.5g | 26g | 0g |

# Conclusion

The Air fryer lets you take all the decadent fried foods you love with a percentage of the calories. Thus, you get all the enjoyment with so much less of what you don't want. Convenience and fun, creativity and innovation, and above all delicious food are inherent in the Air fryer cooking experience when using the recipes contained in this book!

*Note from the author:*
*If you've enjoyed this book, I'd greatly appreciate if you could leave an honest review on Amazon.*
*Reviews are very important to us authors, and it only takes a minute for to post.*
*Thank you*

Made in the USA
Lexington, KY
09 October 2017